Sardinia Travel Guide

Discover the Island of Hidden Gems, Ancient History and Stunning Beaches. Pocket Edition

Ginevra Costa

information is without contract or any type of guarantee assurance.

The trademarks that are used are without any consent, and the publication of the trademark is without permission or backing by the trademark owner. All trademarks and brands within this book are for clarifying purposes only and are the owned by the owners themselves, not affiliated with this document.

TABLE OF CONTENTS

INTRODUCTION: WELCOME TO SARDINIA

Why Sardinia?

Sardinia is a place where time seems to hold its breath, a land that beckons travelers with its raw beauty, enthralling history, and an essence that feels untouched by the rush of modernity. Its allure is not limited to the obvious—its turquoise waters and sun-kissed beaches celebrated in glossy magazines—but extends deep into its rugged mountains, ancient traditions, and the heartbeats of its warm, resilient people. This Mediterranean island is not just a destination; it's a world unto itself, a mosaic of natural wonders and cultural treasures that sets it apart from anywhere else on Earth.

The island's landscapes unfold like a series of paintings, each more vivid than the last. Along the coasts, the sea shimmers in hues so brilliant they seem unreal, from the crystalline blues of Costa Smeralda to the emerald greens of hidden coves accessible only by foot or boat. Sardinia's beaches are rivaled by few, with soft sands and dramatic cliffs that plunge into the waves. Yet, the island's soul is not confined to its shoreline. Venture inland, and the scenery transforms. Rolling hills give way to steep valleys, craggy peaks, and ancient forests. The Gennargentu mountains stand as the island's rugged backbone, their trails inviting hikers to discover Sardinia's untamed beauty. Here, nature thrives in its purest form, free of interference, with wild boar, deer, and golden eagles among its inhabitants.

The island's history is as compelling as its landscapes, a tapestry woven by countless civilizations that have left their mark over thousands of years. Sardinia's story begins in the mists of prehistory, with the enigmatic Nuragic civilization, whose stone towers, or nuraghe, dot the island like silent sentinels. These ancient structures, some over 3,000 years old, bear witness to a culture that remains shrouded in mystery. The Giants of Mont'e Prama, monumental statues unearthed in recent decades, add another layer to this enigma, their purpose and creators still sparking debate among archaeologists. As centuries passed, the island became a crossroads for seafaring powers. Phoenicians, Carthaginians, Romans, Byzantines, and Spanish all left their imprint, from the ruins of Tharros and Nora to the medieval fortresses and churches that rise from Sardinia's towns and hills.

Sardinia's culture, like its history, is distinct and deeply rooted. It is a place where traditions are not relics of the past but living, breathing aspects of daily life. Festivals punctuate the calendar, each a vivid expression of Sardinian identity. The Carnival of Mamoiada, with its eerie masks and costumes, harks back to ancient rites, while the Sagra del Redentore celebrates faith with processions and pageantry. Music and dance remain central to the island's heritage, with haunting melodies played on the launeddas, a traditional wind instrument, and intricate steps performed in folk dances that have been passed down through generations. Sardinia's artisans keep age-old crafts alive, from weaving vibrant textiles to crafting intricate filigree jewelry. These traditions are not displays for tourists; they are threads in the fabric of Sardinian life.

The island's cuisine is another reason it captivates those who visit. Sardinian food is a celebration of its land and sea, a reflection of its geography and history. The flavors are bold and authentic, from the hearty simplicity of pane carasau, a thin, crispy bread, to the rich complexity of porceddu, a slow-roasted suckling pig seasoned with myrtle. Seafood is abundant, with dishes like fregola con arselle, a type of pasta with clams, showcasing the island's maritime bounty. Sardinia is also a paradise for cheese lovers, with pecorino sardo, made from sheep's milk, being a particular highlight. The island's wines, such as the robust Cannonau and the crisp Vermentino, are the perfect accompaniment to its meals. Dining in Sardinia is not just about the food—it's an experience, a ritual that brings people together and embodies the island's hospitality.

Beyond its tangible attractions, Sardinia possesses an intangible magic that leaves an indelible mark on those who visit. It is a place where you can lose yourself in the stillness of an ancient forest or the vastness of a star-studded sky. The island's pace of life invites you to slow down, to savor moments and reconnect with the simple joys of existence. Sardinia's people, known for their warmth and generosity, embody this spirit. Whether sharing a meal, offering directions, or recounting a local legend, their pride in their homeland is evident. It is this human connection that often lingers in the memories of travelers, a reminder that Sardinia is not just a place to see but a place to experience.

The island's diversity ensures there is something for everyone. For adventurers, Sardinia is a playground of possibilities. Its hiking trails, from coastal paths to mountain treks, offer breathtaking views and a sense of discovery. The waters surrounding the island are a haven for snorkeling, diving, and sailing, with marine life as vibrant as the landscapes above. History enthusiasts will find endless fascination in Sardinia's archaeological sites and museums, while those seeking relaxation can bask on its beaches or indulge in the tranquility of its rural retreats. Families, couples, solo travelers—Sardinia welcomes all with open arms, offering experiences that range from the luxurious to the rustic, from the energetic to the serene.

What truly sets Sardinia apart is its authenticity. Despite its popularity as a tourist destination, the island has retained its character and charm. It is a place where you can wander through villages untouched by time, where shepherds still tend their flocks, and where the rhythm of life is dictated by nature rather than the clock. Sardinia is not a place that has been shaped to meet the expectations of visitors; it is a place that invites visitors to immerse themselves in its reality. This authenticity is perhaps its greatest gift, offering a travel experience that feels genuine and deeply enriching.

Sardinia's appeal lies in its ability to surprise and delight at every turn. It is an island of contrasts, where ancient traditions coexist with modern comforts, where wild landscapes give way to refined resorts, and where every corner holds the promise of discovery. It is a destination that defies easy definition, a place that must be experienced to be understood. Sardinia is not just a journey; it is a revelation, a reminder of the beauty and diversity of our world. For those who seek more than a vacation, who yearn for connection and wonder, Sardinia awaits, its treasures ready to be discovered.

How to Use This Guide

This guide has been carefully crafted to help you uncover the best of Sardinia, whether you're a first-time visitor or someone returning to explore its hidden depths. It is designed to be your trusted companion, offering practical advice, detailed insights, and insider tips that cater to a variety of travel styles and preferences. By using this guide effectively, you'll be able to maximize your experience on the island, ensuring that you don't just visit Sardinia but truly connect with it. It is divided into sections that make navigating the wealth of information straightforward while giving you the flexibility to tailor your journey based on your interests, schedule, and budget.

The first step in using this guide is to understand its structure and how it aligns with your needs. Each chapter takes a deep dive into specific aspects of Sardinia, from its captivating history to its stunning beaches, outdoor adventures, and culinary delights. Start by identifying what excites you most about your trip. Are you drawn to the island's ancient ruins and unique culture? Or perhaps you're looking forward to lazy days on pristine beaches paired with evenings indulging in Sardinian cuisine? Pinpointing your priorities will help you focus on the sections most relevant to your trip planning while leaving room for spontaneous exploration once you're on the island.

While it's tempting to read the guide cover to cover, it's not necessary. Think of it as a reference manual that you can dip into as needed. If your trip is still in its early planning stages, you might want to begin with the chapter dedicated to preparation. This section provides crucial advice on the best times to visit Sardinia, how to navigate the island, and what to pack for your adventure. It's particularly useful for understanding the island's unique dynamics, such as the seasonality of certain activities and the practicality of renting a car versus relying on public transportation. Use this information to create a solid foundation for your trip, ensuring that logistical hiccups don't disrupt your experience.

Once the basics are in place, dive into the chapters that detail Sardinia's top destinations. This is where you can start shaping your itinerary, whether you plan to stick to one region or explore the island more widely. Each area is presented with a focus on its unique character, attractions, and practical tips for visitors. For instance, if you're drawn to the glamour of Costa Smeralda, you'll find information on its luxurious resorts, iconic beaches, and vibrant nightlife. On the other hand, if you prefer a quieter, more traditional experience, the guide's insights into towns like Bosa or the rugged interior of Barbagia will steer you in the right direction. Use this section to map out your journey, but remember to leave space for the unexpected. Sardinia has a way of surprising even the most meticulous planners.

The chapter on beaches and coastal escapes is particularly valuable for those seeking sun-drenched relaxation or aquatic adventures. Sardinia's coastline is one of its most celebrated features, but with so many options, choosing the right spots can be overwhelming. This guide breaks it down for you, highlighting both the island's iconic beaches and its lesser-known gems. Whether you're looking for family-friendly sands, secluded coves, or prime locations for snorkeling and diving, this section provides all the details you need to make an informed choice. Keep in mind that some beaches require a bit of effort to reach, so pay attention to the practical advice on accessibility and any necessary preparations.

For history enthusiasts, the chapter on Sardinia's ancient wonders will be indispensable. Use it to uncover the island's rich past, from the mysterious nuraghi to Roman ruins and sacred wells. This section is more than just a list of sites; it offers context and stories that bring these ancient places to life. If you're planning to visit multiple historical locations, consider grouping them geographically to save time and travel costs. The guide also includes tips on what to look for at each site, helping you appreciate the details that might otherwise go unnoticed.

Outdoor adventurers and nature lovers will find their haven in the chapter dedicated to Sardinia's natural attractions. This part of the guide is packed with suggestions for hiking trails, national parks, and other outdoor activities. Use it to plan excursions that match your fitness level and interests, whether that's a challenging trek in the Gennargentu mountains or a leisurely boat tour along the coastline. The guide also provides practical advice for staying safe and respecting the island's natural environment, ensuring that your adventures are both enjoyable and sustainable.

Food and drink are integral to any travel experience, and Sardinia is no exception. The chapter on Sardinian cuisine is your roadmap to the island's culinary landscape. Use it to discover traditional dishes, local wines, and the best places to sample them. Whether you're dining at a high-end restaurant or exploring a bustling market, this section will help you navigate Sardinia's flavors with confidence. Pay attention to the recommendations on food festivals and seasonal specialties, as they offer unique opportunities to immerse yourself in the island's gastronomic culture. This chapter also includes tips on etiquette and customs, ensuring that your dining experiences are as seamless as they are delicious.

As you explore Sardinia, the guide encourages you to go beyond the surface. Take the time to engage with the island's people, whether by participating in local festivals, visiting family-run businesses, or simply striking up a conversation. The guide offers insights into Sardinian customs and ways of life, helping you navigate cultural differences and make meaningful connections. These interactions often become the most memorable parts of a trip, providing a deeper understanding of what makes Sardinia so special.

The guide also includes practical information to help you handle any challenges that may arise during your trip. From tips on avoiding crowded spots during peak season to advice on staying safe in the sun, these details are designed to make your journey as smooth as possible. Use the guide's resources to stay prepared, but don't let minor setbacks dampen your adventure. Sardinia is a place that rewards flexibility and openness, so embrace the unexpected and let the island's charm lead the way.

Finally, don't forget to use the guide's bonus sections to enhance your experience. These features, such as essential travel phrases or printable tools, are designed to make your trip more convenient and enjoyable. They're especially useful for first-time visitors who may feel uncertain about navigating a new destination. Keep these resources handy, as they can save time and effort when you need them most.

This guide is more than just a collection of recommendations; it's a tool to help you create a journey that's uniquely yours. Use it as a starting point, but let your curiosity and instincts shape your adventure. Sardinia is a place of endless possibilities, and this guide is here to ensure that you make the most of every moment. Whether you're seeking relaxation, discovery, or a bit of both, this guide will help you navigate the island with confidence and ease.

A Brief History of Sardinia

Sardinia's history stretches across millennia, a story shaped by the waves of civilizations that have risen and fallen on its rugged terrain. This Mediterranean island has served as a crossroads of cultures, a place where ancient peoples left their marks in stone, metal, and tradition. Today, Sardinia's identity is a blend of these historical layers, each contributing to its unique sense of place. To understand Sardinia fully is to walk through the echoes of its past, from the mysterious nuraghi to the Roman roads, medieval fortresses, and beyond.

Long before recorded history, Sardinia was home to one of Europe's most enigmatic ancient cultures: the Nuragic civilization. Flourishing from roughly 1800 BCE to 200 CE, this society built thousands of stone towers, known as nuraghi, which have become the island's most iconic archaeological feature. These structures, often likened to fortresses or communal hubs, dot the landscape in varying states of preservation, some rising majestically against the horizon while others crumble into the earth. The most famous, Su Nuraxi di Barumini, is a UNESCO World Heritage Site and a testament to the ingenuity of these ancient builders. But the purpose of these towers remains a puzzle. Were they defensive strongholds, places of worship, or centers of governance? The lack of written records has left modern archaeologists to piece together clues, and the mystery only adds to their allure.

The Nuragic people left more than just their towers. Burial sites, sacred wells, and bronze figurines offer glimpses into their spiritual and daily lives. The Giants of Mont'e Prama, massive stone statues discovered in the 1970s, are among their

17

most intriguing legacies. These humanoid figures, with their stylized features and imposing size, remain shrouded in mystery, their exact role in Nuragic society still debated. What is clear is that the Nuragic civilization was highly developed, with a complex social structure and deep connections to the natural world.

As the Nuragic era waned, Sardinia became a point of interest for the seafaring Phoenicians. These traders, hailing from what is now Lebanon, established settlements along the island's coasts around the 9th century BCE. Cities like Tharros, Nora, and Bithia sprang up as hubs of commerce, linking Sardinia to a vast network that stretched across the Mediterranean. The Phoenicians brought with them advanced maritime technology, art, and a system of writing. While their influence was significant, they did not completely displace the indigenous Nuragic culture, which continued to thrive in the island's interior.

The arrival of the Carthaginians in the 6th century BCE marked a new chapter in Sardinia's history. Carthage, a powerful city-state in North Africa, sought to control the island for its strategic location and abundant resources, including metals like copper and lead. The Carthaginians fortified Phoenician settlements and expanded their reach, leaving behind monuments, urban layouts, and artifacts that reflect their sophisticated society. However, their dominance was not uncontested. The indigenous Sardinians resisted, particularly in the mountainous interior, where the rugged terrain provided a natural stronghold. This resistance earned the Sardinians a reputation for fierce independence, a trait that echoes in their modern identity.

Rome's conquest of Sardinia in 238 BCE, following the First Punic War, brought the island under the control of one of history's greatest empires. The Romans valued Sardinia primarily for its grain production, which helped feed their growing population. They established an efficient administrative system, built roads, aqueducts, and other infrastructure, and introduced their language and customs. Roman rule brought a period of relative stability and prosperity, but it also imposed new cultural norms on the Sardinian people. While Roman influence is evident in ruins like the amphitheater in Cagliari and the thermal baths at Fordongianus, the island's interior remained a bastion of traditional ways, resisting full assimilation.

With the decline of the Roman Empire in the 5th century CE, Sardinia entered a turbulent period. The island was briefly controlled by the Vandals, a Germanic tribe who used it as a base for their incursions into the Western Roman Empire. Their rule was short-lived, and by the 6th century, Sardinia had become part of the Byzantine Empire. Under Byzantine rule, the island was organized into administrative districts known as "judicati," a system that would shape its governance for centuries to come. Christianity also became firmly established during this time, leaving a legacy of early churches and religious traditions that persist to this day.

The Middle Ages saw Sardinia fragmented into four autonomous regions, or giudicati, each governed by a judge (giudice). This period of relative independence allowed Sardinia to develop its own governance structures and cultural identity, but it also made the island vulnerable to external threats. The maritime republics of Pisa and Genoa, eager to expand their influence, vied for control of Sardinia. Their rivalry culminated in a series of conflicts that eventually saw the island fall under the dominion of the Crown of Aragon in the 14th century.

The Aragonese period marked a significant turning point. Sardinia became part of the Spanish Empire, a status it would retain for several centuries. Spanish rule brought new architectural styles, language influences, and administrative practices, but it also introduced heavy taxation and feudal oppression. The island's rural population, already marginalized, faced increasing hardship. Despite these challenges, Sardinia's cultural resilience shone through. Traditional music, dance, and crafts flourished, serving as a form of resistance and identity preservation.

In the 18th century, Sardinia's fate shifted once again. Following the War of the Spanish Succession, the island was ceded to the House of Savoy, which later unified Italy. Sardinia played a crucial role in the Risorgimento, the movement for Italian unification, serving as the base for the Kingdom of Sardinia. The island's integration into Italy brought modernization efforts, but it also exposed deep economic and social inequalities. Sardinia remained largely rural and underdeveloped compared to the industrializing mainland, a disparity that fueled emigration and discontent.

The 20th century brought both challenges and opportunities. Sardinia suffered during both World Wars, with its strategic location making it a target for military operations. In the post-war period, efforts to modernize the island gained momentum. Infrastructure projects, tourism development, and cultural initiatives aimed to bridge the gap between Sardinia and mainland Italy. However, these changes also brought tensions, as traditional ways of life clashed with the pressures of modernization.

Today, Sardinia stands as a testament to its rich and varied history. Its past is etched into its landscapes, from the ancient nuraghi to the medieval towers and Spanish-style churches that grace its towns and villages. The island's history is not just a series of events; it's a living legacy that informs its present and shapes its future. Sardinia's ability to adapt while preserving its identity is a testament to the resilience and creativity of its people. Exploring Sardinia's history is not just about visiting sites; it's about understanding the layers of culture, struggle, and triumph that make the island what it is today.

The Unique Culture of Sardinia

Sardinia's culture is a reflection of its geography—a land shaped by isolation, resilience, and a deep connection to its past. Sitting in the heart of the Mediterranean but apart from the mainland, this island has developed traditions, customs, and a way of life that are distinctly its own. Sardinia's unique culture is a mosaic of ancient rituals, linguistic diversity, artisanal craftsmanship, vibrant festivals, and culinary treasures. Every element of this culture tells a story about the island's history and its people, creating an identity that is as rich and multifaceted as its rugged landscapes.

Language plays an essential role in Sardinia's cultural identity. Sardinian, or "Sardu," is not merely a dialect but a language in its own right, with roots in Latin and traces of influences from Phoenician, Arabic, Spanish, and Italian. It is one of the oldest Romance languages in Europe, preserved through centuries of oral tradition. While Italian is the official language, Sardinian is still spoken in many homes and rural communities, serving as a link to the island's past. Variants of Sardinian exist from region to region, and even smaller local dialects add to the linguistic richness. Beyond Sardinian, you'll also encounter Catalan in Alghero, a coastal town where the language has been preserved for centuries due to historical ties with the Kingdom of Aragon. These linguistic layers reveal Sardinia's long history as a crossroads of different civilizations, and the island's commitment to preserving its linguistic heritage speaks volumes about its cultural pride.

The music of Sardinia is unlike anything else in the Mediterranean. One of the most striking examples is the "cantu a tenore," a traditional polyphonic singing style that has been recognized by UNESCO as an intangible cultural heritage of humanity. This ancient form of music is performed by male quartets, with voices echoing the sounds of nature, from the low rumble of the earth to the high-pitched calls of animals. The singers create a haunting, almost otherworldly harmony that feels deeply rooted in Sardinia's landscape. Another musical tradition is the use of the "launeddas," a wind instrument made of cane that dates back over two millennia. Its hypnotic, melodic sound has been a part of Sardinia's celebratory and religious events for centuries. Music is more than just entertainment on the island; it is a form of storytelling, a way of passing down history, and a means of preserving Sardinian identity.

Festivals are at the heart of Sardinian culture, providing a window into the island's rich traditions and communal spirit. These events often blend ancient pagan rituals with Christian customs, creating celebrations that are both unique and

22

deeply rooted in history. One of the most famous is the Carnival of Mamoiada, held in the mountainous Barbagia region. Here, men dressed as "Mamuthones" wear dark wooden masks and heavy cowbells, performing rhythmic, somber dances that harken back to ancient fertility rites or perhaps rituals to ward off evil spirits. In contrast, the "Issohadores," dressed in bright colors, add a lighter, more festive element to the celebration. Another iconic festival is the Sagra del Redentore in Nuoro, where locals don traditional Sardinian costumes and participate in religious processions, music, and dance. Each festival, no matter how small or local, is an opportunity for Sardinians to celebrate their heritage, preserve their customs, and come together as a community.

The island's craftsmanship is another testament to its cultural uniqueness. Sardinian artisans create works that are not only beautiful but also deeply symbolic. Traditional weaving, for example, has been practiced for centuries, with intricate patterns that often have meanings tied to family, nature, or spirituality. These textiles, used as rugs, tapestries, or even ceremonial garments, are a hallmark of Sardinian homes and reflect the island's artistic heritage. Jewelry-making is another revered craft, with gold and silver filigree designs that are delicate yet intricate. These pieces, often passed down through generations, are not just ornaments but also carriers of stories and traditions. Sardinian knives, known for their distinctive curved shapes and detailed handles, are another example of the island's craftsmanship. Originally tools for shepherds, these knives are now highly prized for their artistry and functionality. Each handcrafted item, whether a piece of jewelry or a woven rug, represents the skill, patience, and creativity of Sardinian artisans.

Sardinia's traditional attire is perhaps one of the most visually striking aspects of its culture. Each region of the island has its own variations of traditional dress, which are often worn during festivals and special occasions. These outfits are elaborate and rich in detail, featuring vibrant colors, intricate embroidery, and accessories like jewelry and headdresses. Women's dresses often include layers of skirts, aprons, and bodices, while men's attire typically consists of waistcoats, breeches, and hats. The clothing is not just decorative; it reflects social status, marital status, and regional identity. Wearing these garments is a way for Sardinians to honor their ancestors and keep their cultural heritage alive.

The island's relationship with its land is another cornerstone of its culture. Sardinia has a long history of pastoralism, with sheep farming playing a central role in its economy and way of life. The island's shepherds are not just caretakers of livestock; they are custodians of a lifestyle that has endured for millennia. Their practices are deeply tied to the rhythms of nature, and their knowledge of the land is profound. This connection to the land is also evident in Sardinia's cuisine, which is rooted in local ingredients and traditional methods. The dishes are simple yet flavorful, reflecting the island's agricultural heritage and the creativity of its people in making the most of what the land provides.

Sardinia's spiritual traditions also contribute to its cultural fabric. The island is dotted with churches, sanctuaries, and sacred sites that reflect its deep-seated religiosity. While Christianity is the dominant faith, many Sardinian religious practices have pagan roots. Sacred wells, for example, were places of worship long before the arrival of Christianity, and their significance has persisted in local folklore and traditions.

Pilgrimages to these sites, as well as to Christian sanctuaries like the Basilica of Bonaria in Cagliari, are still common today. These spiritual practices are not just acts of faith; they are communal events that reinforce Sardinian identity and foster a sense of belonging.

Sardinia's culture is also characterized by its hospitality, a value deeply ingrained in its people. Visitors to the island often remark on the warmth and generosity of its inhabitants, who take pride in sharing their traditions, stories, and way of life. This hospitality is evident in the island's food culture, where meals are seen as a time to connect and celebrate. Whether it's a family gathering, a community event, or a simple dinner with friends, Sardinians treat food as more than sustenance—it's an expression of love, gratitude, and tradition. The act of sharing a meal is a cultural ritual that ties people together, creating bonds that transcend time and place.

What makes Sardinia's culture so unique is its ability to balance tradition and modernity. While the island has embraced aspects of the contemporary world, it has done so without losing its roots. Sardinians have found ways to preserve their heritage while adapting to change, ensuring that their culture remains vibrant and relevant. This resilience is a testament to the island's spirit, a quality that has been shaped by centuries of challenges and triumphs. Sardinia's culture is not static; it is a living, breathing entity that continues to evolve while staying true to its essence. It is this dynamic quality that makes Sardinia not just a place to visit, but a place to experience and understand.

CHAPTER 1: PLANNING YOUR TRIP

Best Times to Visit Sardinia

Sardinia's appeal is undeniable year-round, but the island's charm shifts dramatically with the changing seasons. Understanding the best time to visit depends on what you're hoping to experience, whether it's sunbathing on pristine beaches, hiking through rugged mountain trails, exploring ancient ruins, or immersing yourself in the vibrant tapestry of local festivals. Each season offers unique opportunities, and knowing what to expect will help you align your trip with your preferences, making the most of your Sardinian adventure.

Spring in Sardinia, spanning from March to May, is a time of renewal and vibrant beauty. The island comes alive with wildflowers blanketing the countryside, painting the landscapes in vivid hues of red, yellow, and purple. The temperatures during this time are mild and pleasant, typically ranging between 15°C (59°F) and 25°C (77°F). This makes it an ideal season for outdoor activities such as hiking, cycling, and exploring Sardinia's nature reserves. Trails through Gennargentu National Park or along the coast of Ogliastra are particularly inviting, offering breathtaking views without the sweltering heat of summer. Spring also marks the start of Sardinia's festival season, with Easter celebrations like Settimana Santa drawing visitors to towns such as Cagliari and Alghero. These events are steeped in tradition, featuring processions, music, and ceremonies that provide a glimpse into the island's cultural heritage.

For beach lovers, spring offers a quieter alternative to the bustling summer months. While the sea might still be a bit chilly for swimming early in the season, the beaches are tranquil and uncrowded, allowing you to enjoy the stunning coastal scenery in peace. By May, the water begins to warm, and more adventurous travelers can take a dip or try their hand at watersports like kayaking or snorkeling. Additionally, this period is perfect for exploring Sardinia's archaeological sites. The mild weather makes wandering through ancient ruins like those at Nora or Tharros far more enjoyable than under the intense summer sun.

Summer, from June to August, is undoubtedly Sardinia's peak tourist season. During these months, the island transforms into a paradise for beachgoers, with temperatures soaring to an average of 30°C (86°F) and above. The turquoise waters of Sardinia's coastline beckon travelers from around the world, with iconic spots like Costa Smeralda, Cala Luna, and La Pelosa drawing large crowds. If your vision of Sardinia involves lounging on sun-drenched beaches or sailing along its azure waters, summer is the time to visit. Keep in mind, however, that the popularity of this season also means higher prices for accommodations and services, as well as crowded beaches and attractions, particularly in July and August.

Despite the heat, summer is also a season of celebration. Festivals such as Sagra del Redentore in Nuoro and the Festa di Sant'Efisio in Cagliari showcase Sardinia's cultural richness. These events feature traditional costumes, music, dances, and religious processions, offering a chance to witness the island's vibrant community spirit. Nightlife, particularly in coastal towns like Porto Cervo and Alghero, is at its peak, with bars, clubs, and restaurants buzzing with energy. For those seeking a mix of relaxation and excitement, Sardinia in summer delivers an unforgettable experience.

If you plan to visit during this season, it's essential to prepare for the heat. Lightweight clothing, sunscreen, and plenty of water are must-haves. Renting a car is highly recommended, as public transportation can be limited and crowded during the high season. Early planning is also crucial; booking accommodations and activities well in advance will help you secure the best options and avoid disappointment.

Autumn, from September to November, is a hidden gem for travelers seeking a more relaxed and authentic Sardinian experience. The summer crowds begin to disperse, and the island takes on a more serene and introspective atmosphere. Temperatures remain warm, averaging between 20°C (68°F) and 28°C (82°F) in September, making it an excellent time for both beach and outdoor activities. The sea, having been warmed by the summer sun, is still perfect for swimming and watersports, but with far fewer people sharing the shoreline.

Autumn is also a season of harvest, and Sardinia's culinary scene comes to life with food and wine festivals celebrating the island's agricultural bounty. Events such as the Autunno in Barbagia series showcase local specialties, from roasted chestnuts to Cannonau wine, offering visitors a chance to savor Sardinia's traditional flavors. This is an ideal time to explore Sardinia's vineyards and wineries, many of which open their doors to visitors for tastings and tours. The island's markets are brimming with fresh produce, and dining in local trattorias feels even more special as you enjoy dishes made from seasonal ingredients.

For those interested in hiking and exploring Sardinia's natural beauty, autumn is a fantastic season. The cooler temperatures make trekking through the Supramonte mountain range or visiting caves like Grotta di Nettuno more comfortable and enjoyable. Birdwatching is another highlight during this time, as migratory species pass through Sardinia's wetlands and lagoons, creating a spectacle for nature enthusiasts.

Winter in Sardinia, from December to February, may not be the first choice for many travelers, but it holds its own unique charm. While temperatures rarely drop below 5°C (41°F) and average around 10°C to 15°C (50°F to 59°F), the island's atmosphere becomes quieter and more introspective. Sardinia's coastal towns, often bustling in summer, slow down significantly, offering a glimpse into local life without the influence of tourism. This is a time to explore the island's cultural and historical riches at a leisurely pace. Archaeological sites, museums, and churches are far less crowded, allowing for a more intimate experience.

Winter is also the season for experiencing Sardinia's Carnival celebrations, particularly in towns like Mamoiada and Oristano. These events are steeped in tradition, featuring unique masks, costumes, and rituals that harken back to the island's ancient past. The Mamuthones and Issohadores of Mamoiada, for example, are a striking sight, their processions evoking a sense of mystery and connection to Sardinia's roots.

While the beaches may not be the main attraction in winter, the island's interior comes to life. The cooler weather is perfect for exploring Sardinia's villages and countryside, where you'll find warm hospitality and a slower pace of life. This is also a great time to indulge in Sardinia's hearty winter cuisine, with dishes like malloreddus (Sardinian gnocchi) and seadas (a sweet cheese-filled pastry) providing comfort and flavor.

Choosing the best time to visit Sardinia ultimately depends on what you want from your trip. Spring and autumn offer a balance of pleasant weather, fewer crowds, and the chance to experience the island's natural and cultural beauty in a more relaxed setting. Summer is perfect for those seeking vibrant energy, beachside bliss, and lively festivals, while winter provides an opportunity to delve into Sardinia's quieter, more introspective side. Each season brings its own set of experiences, ensuring that no matter when you visit, Sardinia will leave a lasting impression. With careful planning and an understanding of what each season offers, your journey to this extraordinary island will be nothing short of unforgettable.

Transportation on the Island: Renting, Driving, and Public Transit

Navigating Sardinia, a sprawling island with diverse landscapes and scattered attractions, requires careful consideration of transportation options. Its rugged terrain, coastal roads, and remote villages mean that your choice of transport will significantly shape your experience. Sardinia offers a mix of possibilities, from renting a car to relying on public transit or even cycling for the more adventurous. Understanding the pros and cons of each will help you decide what best suits your needs and ensure that you can access the island's treasures efficiently and comfortably.

Renting a car is often the most practical and flexible option for exploring Sardinia, especially if you plan to venture beyond the main cities and tourist hubs. The island's public transportation system, while functional, does not reach many of the more remote or off-the-beaten-path destinations, such as hidden beaches or quaint mountain villages. Having your own vehicle allows you to set your own pace and itinerary, giving you the freedom to stop wherever a scenic vista or charming town catches your eye. Sardinia's roads are generally in good condition, though you'll encounter a mix of wide highways, narrow rural lanes, and winding mountain passes. While some of these roads may seem daunting initially, particularly in the interior regions, they are part of the island's charm and lead to some of its most breathtaking sights.

When renting a car, it's important to book well in advance, especially during the peak summer season, when demand is high, and rental prices can skyrocket. Most major international car rental companies operate at Sardinia's main airports—Cagliari Elmas, Olbia Costa Smeralda, and Alghero Fertilia—as well as in larger towns. Opt for a smaller car if you plan to explore the narrow streets of historic villages or drive along coastal routes where parking can be limited. Many rental agencies offer manual transmission vehicles by default, so if you're more comfortable driving an automatic, be sure to specify this when booking. Additionally, ensure that your rental agreement includes insurance coverage for peace of mind, particularly if you're navigating Sardinia's winding roads for the first time.

Driving in Sardinia is a relatively straightforward experience for those accustomed to European driving norms, though it's worth noting a few key considerations. Traffic is generally light outside of major cities, but urban centers like Cagliari and Olbia can become congested during peak hours. Parking in these cities, as well as in popular tourist areas during the summer, can be challenging, so look for designated lots or garages to avoid fines. In rural areas, be prepared for sharp curves, steep inclines, and the occasional encounter with livestock wandering onto the road. Signage is typically clear, though it's helpful to have a GPS or a reliable map, as cell service can be spotty in remote areas. Speed limits vary depending on the type of road, and local drivers may occasionally interpret them more liberally than visitors are used to, so remaining attentive is essential.

For those who prefer not to drive or are traveling on a tighter budget, Sardinia's public transportation system offers a viable alternative, albeit with limitations. The island's primary modes of public transit are buses and trains, both of which are operated by ARST (Azienda Regionale Sarda Trasporti), the regional transport authority. While the network connects major cities and towns fairly well, reaching smaller villages or more isolated destinations can be challenging. Buses are the more extensive option, with routes covering most of the island, but their schedules can be infrequent, especially in rural areas or on weekends and holidays. Planning your trips around the available timetables is crucial, as missing a bus in a remote area might leave you stranded for hours.

Trains, while less comprehensive than buses, offer a comfortable and scenic way to travel between Sardinia's main cities and certain regional hubs. The Trenitalia-operated network includes routes such as the one between Cagliari and Sassari, which passes through Oristano, and the line connecting Cagliari to Iglesias. Train travel is generally slower than driving but provides a relaxing alternative for those who wish to avoid the stress of navigating unfamiliar roads. Tickets are reasonably priced and can be purchased at stations, online, or through mobile apps. However, as with buses, train services may be reduced during off-peak times, so advance planning is essential.

One of Sardinia's unique transportation experiences is the Trenino Verde, or "Little Green Train," a narrow-gauge railway that offers scenic journeys through the island's interior. Operating mainly during the summer months, this historic train takes passengers through some of Sardinia's most untouched landscapes, including forests, gorges, and rolling hills. While not a practical choice for getting from point A to point B, the Trenino Verde is a memorable way to experience the island's natural beauty and a glimpse into its past.

Taxis and ride-hailing services like Uber are available in Sardinia but are less common than in many other European destinations. Taxis can be found at airports, train stations, and major towns, but they are not typically hailed on the street. Instead, they are booked in advance or through taxi stands. Fares can be expensive, particularly for longer journeys, making them a less practical option for extensive exploration. Ride-hailing apps are limited in their coverage, often restricted to urban areas, so they cannot be relied upon for travel to remote locations.

For travelers who enjoy a slower, more eco-friendly approach, cycling is an increasingly popular way to explore Sardinia. The island's varied terrain offers routes for all skill levels, from gentle coastal paths to challenging mountain climbs. Cycling allows you to immerse yourself in Sardinia's landscapes at a leisurely pace, with the added benefit of being able to stop and appreciate the scenery whenever you like. Many towns and cities have bike rental shops, and some even offer guided cycling tours. However, it's important to be prepared for the island's topography, as steep hills and strong winds can make certain routes demanding. Helmets, proper gear, and a detailed map are essential for a safe and enjoyable ride.

Ferries provide another layer to Sardinia's transportation network, connecting the island to mainland Italy and neighboring Corsica. Major ports like Cagliari, Olbia, and Porto Torres serve as gateways for travelers arriving by sea, as well as for those looking to explore nearby islands such as La Maddalena. Ferries are also a practical option for transporting vehicles, allowing you to combine driving with sea travel. Booking tickets in advance, especially during the busy summer months, ensures availability and often secures better rates.

Ultimately, the best way to navigate Sardinia depends on your itinerary, preferences, and the experiences you seek. Renting a car offers unparalleled freedom and access to the island's hidden gems, while public transit provides a budget-friendly alternative for reaching major destinations. Cycling and ferries add unique perspectives to your journey, allowing you to engage with Sardinia's landscapes and seascapes in a more intimate way. By understanding the strengths and limitations of each option, you can tailor your transportation choices to create a seamless and enriching travel experience. Sardinia's diverse beauty awaits, and the way you move through it will shape how you connect with its many wonders.

Budgeting for Your Sardinian Adventure

Creating a realistic budget for your trip to Sardinia is an essential step in planning and maximizing your experience on this Mediterranean island. Whether you're traveling on a shoestring or indulging in a more luxurious getaway, understanding the costs associated with transportation, accommodations, meals, activities, and other essentials will help you allocate your resources wisely. Sardinia's variety of options, from high-end resorts to modest guesthouses and world-class dining to simple local trattorias, means there's something to suit every budget. Careful planning ensures that you can enjoy the island's highlights without financial surprises along the way.

One of the first expenses to consider is transportation, beginning with how you'll arrive on the island. Flights to Sardinia are available from major European cities, with three main airports—Cagliari, Olbia, and Alghero—serving as entry points. Budget airlines often operate routes to Sardinia, particularly during the summer months, making it possible to secure affordable tickets if you book in advance. Prices can vary significantly depending on the season, with peak summer months seeing higher fares. If you're traveling from mainland Italy, ferries offer an alternative, with prices depending on the route, class of service, and whether you're bringing a vehicle. Including these costs in your initial planning will help create a foundation for your budget.

Once on the island, your choice of transportation will influence your costs further. Renting a car is one of the most convenient ways to explore Sardinia, especially if you plan to visit remote beaches or mountainous regions. Rental prices vary depending on the season and the type of vehicle, with smaller cars typically being more affordable. Fuel costs should also be factored in, as Sardinia's size means you may cover considerable distances during your trip. If you're relying on public transportation, bus and train fares are relatively inexpensive, but you'll need to plan around limited schedules, particularly in rural areas and outside of peak tourist season. Taxis and private transfers, while convenient, can be costly and are best reserved for shorter journeys or when other options are unavailable.

Accommodations will likely be one of the largest components of your budget, and Sardinia offers a wide range of choices to suit different preferences and price points. Luxury travelers will find high-end resorts and boutique hotels, particularly along the Costa Smeralda, where nightly rates can reach hundreds or even thousands of euros during the summer season. For a more budget-friendly option, consider agriturismi—farm stays that offer rustic accommodations and home-cooked meals, often at reasonable prices. Mid-range travelers can choose from privately run bed-and-breakfasts, guesthouses, or small hotels, which provide comfort and convenience without the premium price tag of upscale properties. Booking accommodations well in advance is crucial, especially if you're visiting during the peak summer months when availability diminishes, and prices climb.

Meals are another variable expense that can range from indulgent to economical, depending on where and how you choose to dine. Sardinia is renowned for its culinary traditions, and experiencing the island's flavors is a highlight of any visit. Fine dining establishments, particularly in tourist-heavy areas, can be pricey, with multi-course meals and wine pairings easily costing 50 euros or more per person. However, there are plenty of affordable options to enjoy authentic Sardinian cuisine, including trattorias, osterias, and pizzerias. These establishments often serve hearty portions of local specialties like malloreddus (Sardinian gnocchi) or porceddu (roast suckling pig) at reasonable prices. For those on a tight budget, markets and supermarkets are excellent places to purchase fresh produce, bread, cheese, and cured meats for picnic-style meals. Sampling local street food, such as seadas (a sweet cheese-filled pastry) or panadas (savory pies), is another delicious yet inexpensive way to eat on the go.

Activities and attractions can also vary widely in cost, depending on your interests and itinerary. Many of Sardinia's most stunning sights, such as its beaches and hiking trails, are free to access, making it possible to enjoy the island's natural beauty without spending a fortune. However, some activities, such as guided tours, boat trips, and entrance fees to archaeological sites or museums, come with additional costs. Boat excursions, for example, are a popular way to explore Sardinia's coastline and islands, with prices often ranging from 30 to 100 euros per person, depending on the duration and level of luxury. If you're interested in diving or other water sports, equipment rentals and instructor fees should also be factored into your budget. Planning in advance and prioritizing the activities that matter most to you can help you manage these expenses effectively.

Festivals and cultural events are another way to immerse yourself in Sardinia's traditions without breaking the bank. Many of these events, such as the Carnival of Mamoiada or the Sagra del Redentore, are open to the public and free to attend, offering an opportunity to experience Sardinian culture through music, dance, and processions. While some festivals may include ticketed performances or activities, the overall cost is often minimal compared to the richness of the experience. Additionally, strolling through local markets, visiting historic churches, or exploring small villages can provide meaningful and memorable moments at little to no cost.

Travel insurance is an often-overlooked expense that should be included in your budget. While Sardinia is a relatively safe destination, unexpected events such as medical emergencies, travel delays, or lost luggage can disrupt even the best-planned trips. Comprehensive travel insurance provides peace of mind and financial protection, ensuring that you're covered in case of unforeseen circumstances. Policies vary in price, so it's worth shopping around to find one that meets your needs and fits within your budget.

Tipping is not customary in Sardinia to the extent it is in some other countries, but rounding up the bill or leaving a small amount of change as a gesture of appreciation for good service is common practice. This applies to restaurants, taxis, and other service providers. While tipping won't significantly impact your budget, it's helpful to be aware of local customs to avoid over- or under-tipping during your trip.

Souvenirs and shopping are additional expenses that can vary depending on your interests and preferences. Sardinia is known for its artisanal crafts, including handwoven textiles, ceramics, and jewelry, which make for unique and meaningful keepsakes. While high-quality items may come with a higher price tag, purchasing directly from local artisans or markets often ensures better value and supports the island's traditional crafts. Budgeting a small amount for souvenirs allows you to bring a piece of Sardinia home without overspending.

One way to manage your budget effectively is to divide it into daily allocations, accounting for expected expenses such as meals, transportation, and activities. This approach helps you monitor your spending and make adjustments as needed.

Keeping track of your expenses throughout your trip, whether through a travel app or a simple notebook, ensures that you stay within your limits while still enjoying the experiences that matter most to you.

Sardinia's diverse offerings mean that it's possible to enjoy the island on a wide range of budgets, from backpackers seeking affordable adventures to luxury travelers indulging in the best the island has to offer. By planning ahead, prioritizing your expenses, and making informed choices, you can create a travel experience that aligns with your financial goals while still capturing the essence of Sardinia's beauty, culture, and charm. Whether you're savoring a gourmet meal overlooking the turquoise sea or discovering an ancient ruin on a shoestring budget, Sardinia promises a journey that is as enriching as it is unforgettable.

Packing Tips: Essentials for Every Traveler

Packing for a trip to Sardinia requires careful consideration due to the island's diverse landscapes, varying climates, and the wide range of activities it offers. From pristine beaches to rugged mountain trails, historical landmarks to bustling markets, Sardinia's attractions call for a versatile wardrobe and well-planned essentials. Packing the right items not only ensures your comfort but also allows you to adapt seamlessly to the island's rhythms. By focusing on practical essentials and avoiding unnecessary bulk, you'll be prepared to make the most of your journey.

The foundation of any well-packed suitcase begins with understanding Sardinia's climate and the season in which you plan to visit. Summers are hot and dry, with temperatures often exceeding 30°C (86°F), particularly in July and August. Light, breathable clothing made from natural fabrics like cotton or linen is essential to stay cool during the day. A wide-brimmed hat or a lightweight cap, along with sunglasses with UV protection, will shield you from the strong Mediterranean sun. Don't forget to pack sunscreen with a high SPF rating— preferably water-resistant—to protect your skin during outdoor activities or while lounging on the beach. If you're visiting in spring or autumn, when temperatures are milder, layering becomes important. Lightweight jackets, cardigans, or long-sleeve shirts can help you adapt to cooler mornings and evenings. Winter, though relatively mild compared to mainland Europe, can still bring chilly winds and occasional rain, especially in the mountainous regions. A waterproof jacket and a warm sweater are must-haves if traveling during this season.

Footwear deserves special attention, as Sardinia's terrain varies significantly depending on where you go. For days spent exploring historic towns or strolling through markets, comfortable walking shoes or sandals with good arch support are invaluable. If you plan to hike in the island's nature reserves or trek through archaeological sites like Tiscali or Su Nuraxi, sturdy hiking boots or trail shoes are essential to navigate uneven surfaces and rocky paths. Beaches, on the other hand, often feature coarse sand or pebbly shores, so bringing water shoes can make swimming and walking along the coast more comfortable. For evenings out, especially in more upscale areas like Costa Smeralda, a pair of stylish but comfortable shoes will suit Sardinia's relaxed yet elegant vibe.

Swimwear is a non-negotiable item for a trip to Sardinia, renowned for its crystal-clear waters and stunning beaches. Pack at least two or three swimsuits to rotate during your stay, giving you flexibility while others dry. A lightweight, quick-drying towel is also a great addition, particularly if you're planning to explore multiple beaches in a single day. Many Sardinian beaches lack amenities like loungers or umbrellas, so a compact beach mat and a portable umbrella or sunshade can enhance your comfort during long days by the sea. For snorkeling enthusiasts, bringing your own mask, snorkel, and fins can save rental costs and allow you to explore the underwater world at your leisure.

Sardinia's vibrant towns and picturesque villages often call for casual yet presentable attire, especially when dining out or attending local festivals. While the island's atmosphere is laid-back, certain establishments and events may have a smart-casual dress code. For men, a lightweight button-up shirt paired with chinos or tailored shorts works well, while women might opt for a breezy sundress or a blouse with flowy trousers. Neutral colors and simple patterns are versatile choices that can be mixed and matched effortlessly. A lightweight scarf or shawl is a versatile accessory that not only adds a touch of style but also serves practical purposes, such as covering your shoulders when visiting religious sites or providing warmth on cool evenings.

A well-organized daypack or small backpack is indispensable for daily outings in Sardinia, whether you're hiking, sightseeing, or heading to the beach. Choose one with multiple compartments to keep items like your wallet, phone, camera, and snacks easily accessible. A reusable water bottle is a must, as staying hydrated is crucial under the Sardinian sun. Many towns have public fountains with drinkable water, so carrying a refillable bottle not only saves money but also reduces plastic waste. For tech-savvy travelers, a portable charger or power bank ensures that your devices stay powered throughout the day, especially when navigating with GPS or capturing memorable moments on your phone or camera.

Sardinia's rich cultural and historical heritage means that you'll likely spend time exploring museums, archaeological sites, and traditional villages. A lightweight guidebook or a digital travel app can enhance your experience by providing context and insights into the places you visit. However, if you prefer to disconnect from technology and immerse yourself fully in the surroundings, a small notebook and pen can be useful for jotting down observations, sketching, or recording highlights of your trip. Binoculars are another thoughtful addition, particularly for birdwatchers or anyone interested in observing Sardinia's diverse flora and fauna.

Practical items like a compact first-aid kit, insect repellent, and any necessary medications should not be overlooked. Sardinia's natural beauty often comes with mosquitos, especially in the evenings or near wetlands, so packing an effective bug spray can save you from discomfort. If you're prone to motion sickness, consider bringing remedies for ferry rides or winding mountain roads. Travelers with dietary restrictions or allergies may also benefit from carrying a small supply of snacks or specialty items, as some rural areas may have limited options.

For longer stays or trips that involve a mix of activities, packing cubes can help keep your luggage organized and make it easier to find specific items quickly. Separating clothes by type—such as beachwear, casual outfits, and hiking gear—

saves time and reduces stress when you're on the go. A lightweight laundry bag or a few resealable plastic bags are also handy for separating dirty or wet clothing from the rest of your belongings.

Documentation is another critical aspect of packing, and ensuring that you have all necessary papers organized will streamline your travel experience. Your passport, driver's license (if you plan to rent a car), travel insurance details, and any reservation confirmations should be kept in a secure, easily accessible location, such as a travel wallet or document organizer. It's a good idea to carry both physical copies and digital backups of important documents, such as scanning them to your phone or storing them in cloud storage. This precaution ensures that you're prepared for any unexpected situations.

Sardinia's charm lies in its unpredictability and the sense of adventure it inspires, so packing items that allow for spontaneity is always a good idea. A deck of cards or a small travel game can provide entertainment during downtime, while a collapsible tote bag is perfect for impromptu shopping at local markets or carrying extra items on day trips. If you're a photography enthusiast, consider bringing additional memory cards or spare batteries for your camera to capture Sardinia's stunning landscapes without interruption.

When packing for Sardinia, striking a balance between essentials and versatility is key. The goal is to be prepared for the island's diverse offerings without overloading yourself with unnecessary items. By considering the activities you'll engage in, the season of your visit, and your personal preferences, you can create a packing list that ensures your comfort and enhances your experience. Sardinia rewards those who come prepared, offering a journey filled with beauty, culture, and unforgettable moments that require only the right essentials to fully enjoy.

CHAPTER 2: SARDINIA'S TOP DESTINATIONS

Cagliari: The Bustling Capital

Cagliari, Sardinia's vibrant capital, is a city that weaves together layers of history, culture, and modernity into a seamless experience. Perched along the southern coast and overlooking the expansive Gulf of Angels, it serves as both a bustling metropolitan hub and a gateway to the island's rich heritage. Its narrow streets, sun-drenched piazzas, ancient ruins, and lively markets create a cityscape that balances tradition with contemporary charm. Exploring Cagliari reveals its soul—a city shaped by centuries of Mediterranean influences but proudly distinct in its identity.

One of the first things that strikes visitors is Cagliari's dramatic setting. The city sprawls across seven hills, offering panoramic views at nearly every turn. From the moment you arrive, whether by air or sea, the sight of its terracotta rooftops cascading down to the azure waters of the Mediterranean is captivating. The port, with its constant hum of ferries, fishing boats, and yachts, anchors the city to the sea. As Sardinia's main entry point for many travelers, Cagliari welcomes visitors with an energy that hints at the stories waiting to be discovered within.

The historic heart of the city lies in Castello, a medieval quarter perched atop one of the hills. Wandering through its labyrinth of cobblestone streets feels like stepping back in time. This area, once the stronghold of the Pisans and later the Spanish, is a treasure trove of architectural gems. The imposing Torre di San Pancrazio and Torre dell'Elefante, two massive stone towers, stand as reminders of the city's fortified past. From these vantage points, you can gaze out over the city below, the harbor, and the distant horizon. Within Castello, the Cathedral of Santa Maria is a must-visit. Its ornate façade and richly decorated interior, featuring a mix of Gothic, Baroque, and Romanesque styles, reflect the layered history of the city. The crypt, with its intricately carved columns, adds an air of quiet reverence to the experience.

Descending from Castello, you'll find yourself in the Marina district, a lively area that reflects Cagliari's maritime heritage. This neighborhood, nestled close to the port, is a hub of restaurants, cafes, and boutiques. The aroma of seafood wafts through the air as you stroll past trattorias offering dishes like fregola with clams or fresh grilled fish. This is the perfect place to pause and enjoy a leisurely meal, accompanied by a glass of Vermentino or Cannonau, two of Sardinia's celebrated wines. The Marina district also offers a glimpse into Sardinia's modern side, with its chic stores and vibrant nightlife, where locals and visitors mingle effortlessly.

The city's markets are another highlight, and none is more iconic than Mercato di San Benedetto. As one of the largest covered markets in Europe, it's a feast for the senses. The ground floor is dedicated to seafood, with stalls overflowing with freshly caught fish, octopus, and shellfish. Upstairs, you'll find an array of local produce, cheeses, cured meats, and baked goods. Sampling Sardinian pecorino cheese or a slice of pane carasau (thin, crispy bread) is a simple yet unforgettable way to connect with the island's culinary traditions. The market is not just a place to shop but a social hub, where you can observe the rhythms of daily life and interact with the friendly vendors who are eager to share their knowledge.

Cagliari's connection to its ancient past is evident in its archaeological sites, which offer windows into civilizations that once thrived here. The Roman Amphitheater, carved directly into the limestone hillside, is one of the city's most impressive landmarks. Once a venue for gladiatorial games and public spectacles, the amphitheater now serves as a backdrop for concerts and cultural events, blending antiquity with modern artistic expression. Nearby, the Museo Archeologico Nazionale houses an extensive collection of artifacts, including bronze statuettes from the Nuragic civilization, Phoenician relics, and Roman mosaics. This museum provides invaluable context for understanding the island's history and the various cultures that have shaped it.

Nature is never far from reach in Cagliari, making it a city where urban life and the outdoors harmoniously coexist. The Molentargius-Saline Regional Park, located just a short distance from the city center, is a haven for wildlife enthusiasts. This wetland area is home to a variety of bird species, including the iconic pink flamingos that have become synonymous with the park. Walking or cycling along its trails offers a peaceful escape from the city's bustle, with the shimmering salt flats providing a unique and tranquil backdrop.

Of course, no visit to Cagliari would be complete without experiencing its beaches. Poetto Beach, stretching for nearly eight kilometers, is the city's most famous stretch of sand. Its lively promenade is lined with beach bars, restaurants, and kiosks, making it a popular spot for both locals and tourists. Whether you're basking in the sun, swimming in the clear waters, or enjoying an aperitivo as the sun sets, Poetto embodies the relaxed Mediterranean lifestyle. For those seeking a quieter experience, Cala Mosca and Calamosca are smaller, more secluded beaches that offer a calm retreat.

Cagliari's cultural calendar is filled with events and festivals that showcase its traditions and spirit. One of the most significant is the Festa di Sant'Efisio, held every May. This religious procession, which honors the city's patron saint, is a stunning display of devotion and community. Participants dressed in traditional Sardinian attire parade through the streets, accompanied by music, flower-decorated carts, and oxen. The festival, which dates back to the 17th century, culminates in a journey to the nearby town of Nora, where the saint is believed to have been martyred. Attending this event provides a deep insight into Sardinia's culture and the enduring importance of its religious traditions.

For art and history enthusiasts, Cagliari offers a range of museums and galleries that delve into the island's heritage and contemporary creativity. The Pinacoteca Nazionale di Cagliari, located within the Citadel of Museums, features works by Sardinian and Italian artists, including religious paintings and medieval artifacts. Meanwhile, contemporary art lovers will appreciate the exhibitions at the Galleria Comunale d'Arte, set within the lush Giardini Pubblici. These cultural spaces highlight the breadth of Sardinia's artistic expression, from its ancient origins to its modern interpretations.

Cagliari's neighborhoods each have their own character and charm, inviting exploration beyond the main tourist areas. Villanova, with its pastel-colored houses and flower-filled balconies, is a picturesque quarter that feels like a village within the city. The streets are quieter here, making it an ideal place for a leisurely wander or a coffee break at a local café.

Stampace, another historic district, is known for its churches and traditional shops, offering a more intimate glimpse into Cagliari's everyday life. Each neighborhood adds a layer to the city's identity, encouraging visitors to delve deeper and discover its many facets.

The rhythm of life in Cagliari is infectious, blending the energy of a modern capital with the laid-back charm of the Mediterranean. It's a city that invites you to slow down, savor its flavors, and immerse yourself in its stories. Whether you're marveling at ancient ruins, savoring fresh seafood by the harbor, or watching the flamingos at sunset, Cagliari leaves an impression that lingers long after you've left. It's a place where history and modernity coexist effortlessly, offering a rich tapestry of experiences that capture the essence of Sardinia.

Costa Smeralda: The Luxury Playground

Costa Smeralda, a glittering jewel along Sardinia's northeastern coast, is synonymous with luxury, sophistication, and breathtaking natural beauty. This elite destination, renowned for its pristine beaches and turquoise waters, has long been a magnet for the world's wealthy and glamorous. Yet, Costa Smeralda is more than just a playground for the rich—it is a region that balances exclusivity with a profound connection to its surroundings, offering travelers a taste of indulgence alongside the untamed charm of Sardinia's coastline. Whether you're drawn by the allure of high-end resorts, designer boutiques, or the chance to experience one of the most stunning landscapes in the Mediterranean, Costa Smeralda delivers an unforgettable escape.

The story of Costa Smeralda begins in the early 1960s, when a consortium of international investors, led by Prince Karim Aga Khan IV, recognized the potential of this unspoiled stretch of coastline. At the time, the area was largely undeveloped, its rocky shores and secluded bays known only to shepherds and fishermen. The prince envisioned a destination that would rival the French Riviera, combining exclusive luxury with the natural beauty of Sardinia. From this vision, Costa Smeralda was born, its name meaning "Emerald Coast" in reference to the vivid green hue of the sea. The development was carefully planned to harmonize with the landscape, with architects and designers incorporating traditional Sardinian elements into the region's signature style. Today, Costa Smeralda remains a testament to this vision, a place where glamour meets the timeless allure of nature.

One of the most iconic destinations within Costa Smeralda is Porto Cervo, the heart of the region and a symbol of its opulence. This charming village, designed by architect Luigi Vietti, is a masterpiece of Mediterranean architecture, with its whitewashed buildings, terracotta roofs, and winding streets. The village overlooks a stunning natural harbor, where luxury yachts from around the world anchor, creating a scene that is as captivating as it is extravagant. Porto Cervo is home to high-end boutiques, art galleries, and gourmet restaurants, making it a paradise for those seeking indulgence. Strolling through its Piazzetta, you'll find flagship stores from renowned brands such as Gucci, Prada, and Louis Vuitton, alongside local artisans showcasing Sardinian craftsmanship. Even if you're not planning to splurge, the atmosphere of Porto Cervo is a spectacle in itself, offering a glimpse into the lifestyles of its glamorous visitors.

Beyond the village, Costa Smeralda's beaches are the true stars of the region. Each stretch of sand seems to outdo the last, with Cala di Volpe, Liscia Ruja, and Spiaggia del Principe among the most famous. These beaches, framed by granite rocks and lush vegetation, are celebrated for their powdery white sand and crystal-clear waters. Spiaggia del Principe, in particular, is often hailed as one of the most beautiful beaches in the Mediterranean, its name deriving from Prince Aga Khan's fondness for it. Whether you choose to bask in the sun, swim in the calm waters, or explore the underwater world through snorkeling or diving, the beaches of Costa Smeralda promise moments of pure serenity.

The region's connection to the sea extends beyond its beaches. Sailing is a quintessential part of the Costa Smeralda experience, with regattas and yacht races attracting enthusiasts from around the globe. The Yacht Club Costa Smeralda, founded in 1967 by Prince Aga Khan, is a prestigious institution that hosts some of the most important events in the sailing calendar, such as the Rolex Swan Cup and the Loro Piana Superyacht Regatta. Even if you're not a sailor, the sight of elegant vessels gliding across the water is a captivating addition to the coastal scenery. For those who wish to experience life on the open sea, boat rentals and private charters offer the opportunity to explore hidden coves, remote islands, and the sparkling waters of the archipelago.

While Costa Smeralda is often associated with luxury, it also offers glimpses of Sardinia's rich cultural heritage. The nearby Nuraghe Albucciu and the Giants' Tomb of Coddu Vecchiu are reminders of the island's ancient Nuragic civilization, which flourished thousands of years ago. These archaeological sites provide a fascinating contrast to the modern opulence of the region, connecting visitors to a history that predates the Roman Empire. Local traditions are also celebrated through festivals and events, such as the Arzachena Summer Festival, which features music, dance, and crafts that showcase the island's unique identity.

Dining in Costa Smeralda is an experience that combines world-class cuisine with the flavors of Sardinia. The region is home to some of the island's most acclaimed restaurants, where chefs blend traditional recipes with innovative techniques. Fresh seafood takes center stage on many menus, with dishes like bottarga (cured mullet roe), fregola with clams, and grilled octopus showcasing the bounty of the Mediterranean. Pairing these dishes with Sardinian wines, such as Vermentino di Gallura or Cannonau, elevates the dining experience further. For those seeking a more casual meal, local trattorias and beachside cafes offer delicious options without the formality of fine dining, ensuring that every palate is satisfied.

Accommodations in Costa Smeralda range from lavish resorts to boutique hotels, each offering a unique take on Sardinian hospitality. The Hotel Cala di Volpe, with its iconic architecture and celebrity clientele, is one of the most famous properties in the region, epitomizing luxury and exclusivity. Meanwhile, smaller establishments like Relais Villa del Golfo provide an intimate atmosphere, blending elegance with personalized service. No matter where you stay, the emphasis is on comfort, style, and a deep connection to the surrounding landscape.

For those looking to venture beyond the main attractions, the surrounding areas of Costa Smeralda offer hidden treasures waiting to be discovered. The Maddalena Archipelago, a cluster of islands just off the coast, is a UNESCO World Heritage site renowned for its untouched beauty. A boat trip through the archipelago reveals secluded beaches, turquoise lagoons, and dramatic cliffs that seem to rise from the sea. The island of Caprera, part of the archipelago, is particularly notable as the home of Giuseppe Garibaldi, one of Italy's most revered historical figures. His house, now a museum, offers insights into his life and legacy, adding a layer of historical depth to the natural splendor of the area.

Despite its reputation for exclusivity, Costa Smeralda remains accessible to travelers with a range of budgets. While high-end experiences dominate the region, there are opportunities to enjoy its beauty without breaking the bank. Visiting during the shoulder seasons of spring and autumn allows you to experience the region with fewer crowds and lower prices, while still enjoying warm weather and stunning scenery. Exploring public beaches, dining at local trattorias, and staying in nearby towns like Arzachena or Cannigione can also provide a more affordable way to experience the magic of Costa Smeralda.

What makes Costa Smeralda truly special is its ability to blend luxury with authenticity. While it dazzles with its high-end offerings, it never loses sight of the natural and cultural riches that make Sardinia unique. From the sparkling waters and golden sands to the echoes of ancient history and the warmth of Sardinian hospitality, Costa Smeralda invites you to indulge, explore, and create memories that will last a lifetime. Whether you arrive seeking relaxation, adventure, or a taste of the high life, this remarkable corner of Sardinia promises an experience that transcends expectations.

Alghero: A Medieval Coastal Gem

Alghero, a captivating medieval town on Sardinia's northwestern coast, is a place where history, culture, and natural beauty converge. Known as the "Little Barcelona" due to its strong Catalan influence, this coastal gem boasts a distinctive identity shaped by centuries of diverse rulers, from the Genoese to the Catalans and beyond. Its cobblestone streets, fortified walls, Gothic architecture, and azure waters create an enchanting atmosphere that invites exploration at every turn. Alghero is not only a destination for those seeking history and charm but also a gateway to some of Sardinia's most stunning landscapes and experiences. Whether you're wandering through its old town or venturing into the surrounding countryside, Alghero offers a journey through time and tradition.

The old town of Alghero, or "Centro Storico," is the beating heart of the city and a must-visit for anyone stepping foot in the area. Encircled by ancient walls and overlooking the shimmering Mediterranean, this historic quarter is a labyrinth of narrow streets lined with ochre-colored buildings, boutique shops, and inviting cafes. Walking through these streets feels like being transported to another era, where remnants of the past coexist with modern life. The Catalan Gothic architecture, a legacy of the Aragonese rule during the 14th century, is evident in landmarks such as the Cathedral of Santa Maria. This imposing structure, with its ornate rose window and bell tower, reflects the unique blend of Sardinian and Catalan styles that define Alghero's character. Inside, the cathedral's chapels and intricate details offer a quiet space for reflection and admiration.

The waterfront promenade, known as the "Bastioni," is one of Alghero's most iconic features. Stretching along the old town's fortifications, the Bastioni offer sweeping views of the sea and the distant Capo Caccia cliffs. As you stroll along this path, you'll pass cannons, watchtowers, and stone walls that once defended the city from invaders. Today, the Bastioni are a place of tranquility, where locals and visitors alike gather to enjoy the sunset or sip a glass of wine at one of the many terrace bars overlooking the water. The contrast between the ancient stones and the vibrant Mediterranean scenery creates a setting that is both timeless and invigorating.

Alghero's ties to Catalonia are not only architectural but also cultural. The local dialect, Algherese, is a variant of Catalan, and the influence is evident in the town's traditions, cuisine, and even street signs. This connection is celebrated through festivals and events, such as the Festa di San Michele, honoring the town's patron saint. During this time, Alghero comes alive with music, processions, and cultural performances that highlight its unique heritage. Witnessing these events provides a deeper understanding of the town's identity and the resilience of its traditions.

The culinary scene in Alghero is another highlight, offering a fusion of Sardinian and Catalan flavors that delight the senses. Seafood takes center stage, with dishes like Aragosta alla Catalana (Catalan-style lobster) showcasing the town's maritime heritage. This delicacy, often served with a simple dressing of olive oil, lemon, and tomatoes, is a testament to the quality and freshness of Alghero's ingredients. Other must-try dishes include spaghetti with sea urchin, fregola with clams, and bottarga, a cured fish roe known as "Sardinian caviar." For dessert, seadas—deep-fried pastries filled with cheese and drizzled with honey—offer a sweet ending to any meal. Pairing these dishes with a glass of Vermentino or Torbato, a wine unique to the region, enhances the dining experience further.

Beyond the town itself, Alghero serves as a gateway to some of Sardinia's most breathtaking natural wonders. The Capo Caccia promontory, with its dramatic cliffs plunging into the sea, is a sight to behold. This area is home to the famous Neptune's Grotto, a stunning sea cave adorned with stalactites and stalagmites. Accessible by boat or via a steep staircase known as the Escala del Cabirol, the grotto is a testament to the island's geological beauty. Exploring its chambers and formations feels like stepping into an otherworldly realm, where nature's artistry takes center stage.

For those who prefer the open-air, the Porto Conte Natural Park offers a haven of biodiversity and outdoor activities. This protected area, encompassing forests, wetlands, and coastline, is ideal for hiking, birdwatching, and cycling. Trails within the park lead to panoramic viewpoints, where you can take in the rugged beauty of the landscape and the sparkling sea beyond. The park's commitment to preserving its environment ensures that visitors can connect with nature in its purest form.

Alghero's beaches are another draw, with their golden sands and crystalline waters providing the perfect setting for relaxation. Spiaggia di Maria Pia, located just a short distance from the town center, is a favorite among families for its shallow waters and soft sand. Further afield, beaches like Mugoni and Porto Ferro offer a more secluded experience, surrounded by pine forests and dunes. The variety of beaches near Alghero ensures that every visitor can find their ideal spot, whether it's for sunbathing, snorkeling, or simply enjoying the sound of the waves.

The nearby Nuraghe Palmavera, an archaeological site dating back to the Nuragic civilization, offers a glimpse into Sardinia's ancient history. This complex, consisting of stone towers and village ruins, provides insight into the island's prehistoric culture and the ingenuity of its early inhabitants. Walking among these structures, you can't help but marvel at the connection between Sardinia's distant past and the vibrant life of Alghero today.

Shopping in Alghero is an experience that combines local craftsmanship with modern sophistication. The town is particularly known for its coral jewelry, made from the red coral harvested along its coast. Artisans transform this precious material into intricate necklaces, earrings, and bracelets, which make for unique and meaningful souvenirs. Other local products, such as handmade ceramics, textiles, and Sardinian wines, reflect the island's rich traditions and are readily available in the town's boutiques and markets.

The rhythm of life in Alghero is both relaxed and vibrant, inviting visitors to slow down and savor its many offerings. Whether you're sipping an espresso at a café in Piazza Civica, exploring the bustling market stalls, or watching fishing boats return to the harbor, there's a sense of connection to the town's history and its people. Alghero's ability to blend its medieval charm with modern comforts makes it a destination that appeals to a wide range of travelers, from history enthusiasts to beach lovers and foodies.

Evenings in Alghero are a magical time, as the town takes on a golden glow under the setting sun. The streets come alive with the sounds of laughter and clinking glasses, as locals and visitors gather to enjoy aperitifs and dine al fresco. The sense of community is palpable, creating an atmosphere that is as welcoming as it is enchanting. Whether you choose to linger over a long meal or take a leisurely stroll along the Bastioni, the evenings in Alghero leave a lasting impression.

Alghero's charm lies in its ability to transport you through time while grounding you in the beauty of the present. It is a place where the past and the present coexist harmoniously, offering a rich tapestry of experiences that capture the essence of Sardinia. Whether you're discovering its historic streets, indulging in its culinary delights, or marveling at its natural wonders, Alghero leaves an indelible mark on all who visit. It is a destination that invites you to immerse yourself fully, to embrace its stories, and to take a piece of its spirit with you wherever you go.

Olbia: Gateway to the North

Olbia, nestled along Sardinia's northeastern coast, serves as the island's vibrant gateway to the north. While often regarded as a transit point thanks to its bustling port and airport, Olbia is much more than just an entryway. It is a city with a soul, blending modern conveniences with ancient history, natural beauty, and a rich cultural heritage. Its strategic location makes it the perfect launching pad for exploring the glamorous Costa Smeralda, the rugged hinterlands, and the pristine islands of the Maddalena Archipelago. But before rushing off to these iconic destinations, Olbia itself deserves attention, offering a tapestry of experiences that will reveal Sardinia's unique charm.

The first thing that strikes you upon arriving in Olbia is its energy. The city pulses with life, its streets bustling with locals and travelers alike. Corso Umberto I, the main thoroughfare, is the beating heart of the town. Lined with cafes, boutiques, and restaurants, it invites you to slow down and savor the atmosphere. Whether you're sipping a cappuccino at a sidewalk table or browsing the shops for locally crafted goods, the street has a way of drawing you into its rhythm. At night, the energy shifts as the street comes alive with twinkling lights and the murmur of laughter, creating a warm and inviting ambiance.

Olbia's history stretches back thousands of years, and evidence of its ancient roots can be found throughout the city. The Basilica of San Simplicio is one of its most significant landmarks, a Romanesque church that dates to the 11th century. Built from granite and perched on a slight hill, the basilica is both austere and beautiful, a testament to Sardinia's early Christian heritage. Inside, its simplicity belies the depth of its history, with faded frescoes and ancient inscriptions that hint at the lives of those who worshipped here centuries ago. Each year, the Festa di San Simplicio, held in honor of the city's patron saint, transforms the area around the basilica into a vibrant celebration filled with processions, music, and traditional Sardinian food.

For those intrigued by Sardinia's prehistoric past, a visit to the nearby Nuraghe Riu Mulinu offers a fascinating glimpse into the island's ancient civilizations. This archaeological site, located on a hill overlooking Olbia, is part of the Nuragic network of stone towers that dot Sardinia's landscape. Walking among the remnants of the nuraghe, you can imagine the lives of the people who once inhabited this area, their connection to the land, and the mysteries of their culture. The panoramic views from the site, stretching out over the city and the shimmering Gulf of Olbia, add to the sense of timelessness.

The waterfront is another defining feature of Olbia, and it plays a central role in the city's identity. The port, one of the busiest in Sardinia, is a hive of activity, with ferries arriving and departing for destinations across the Mediterranean. Strolling along the promenade, you'll see fishing boats bobbing alongside luxury yachts, a juxtaposition that reflects Olbia's blend of tradition and modernity. The Lungomare, a recently revitalized area, offers a pleasant space for walking, jogging, or simply enjoying the sea breeze. The waterfront also hosts events and festivals throughout the year, adding to its dynamic appeal.

Olbia's culinary scene is a celebration of Sardinian flavors, with an emphasis on fresh, locally sourced ingredients. Seafood is a highlight, and dishes like spaghetti alle vongole (spaghetti with clams) or zuppa di pesce (fish soup) are must-tries for any visitor. Traditional Sardinian fare, such as malloreddus (a type of gnocchi) or porceddu (roast suckling pig), is also widely available, reflecting the island's agricultural roots. The city's many restaurants and trattorias cater to a range of tastes and budgets, from casual eateries serving hearty portions to fine dining establishments offering innovative takes on regional cuisine. Pairing your meal with a glass of Vermentino, a crisp white wine from the surrounding Gallura region, enhances the experience and provides a true taste of the local terroir.

For a deeper dive into Sardinia's winemaking traditions, a visit to one of the nearby vineyards is highly recommended. The

Gallura region, of which Olbia is a part, is renowned for its Vermentino di Gallura, the island's only DOCG wine. Many wineries offer tours and tastings, where you can learn about the winemaking process and the unique characteristics of the region's terroir. Sipping a glass of Vermentino while overlooking the sunlit vineyards is an experience that captures the essence of Sardinia's lifestyle.

Nature enthusiasts will find plenty to explore in and around Olbia. Just a short drive from the city, the Tavolara-Punta Coda Cavallo Marine Protected Area is a paradise for outdoor activities. This area, encompassing dramatic cliffs, crystal-clear waters, and secluded coves, is perfect for snorkeling, diving, or kayaking. The island of Tavolara, a towering limestone massif rising from the sea, is a striking focal point of the area and offers hiking trails with breathtaking views. The marine reserve's biodiversity and pristine environment make it a haven for anyone seeking a connection with nature.

Beaches near Olbia are as diverse as they are beautiful, ranging from family-friendly stretches of sand to hidden gems tucked away along the coast. Pittulongu Beach, just a few kilometers from the city, is a favorite among locals for its soft sand and shallow waters, making it ideal for families with young children. Further afield, beaches like Cala Brandinchi and Lu Impostu, often referred to as "Tahiti" for their Caribbean-like waters, offer a more tranquil escape. These beaches, with their powdery sand and turquoise seas, are a reminder of why Sardinia is considered one of the world's top beach destinations.

Shopping in Olbia offers a mix of modern retail and traditional craftsmanship. The city's boutiques and markets showcase Sardinian textiles, ceramics, jewelry, and other artisanal goods that make for meaningful souvenirs. The weekly market, held in Piazza Crispi, is a lively affair where you can browse stalls selling everything from fresh produce to handmade crafts. Whether you're looking for a unique keepsake or simply soaking up the atmosphere, the market provides a glimpse into the everyday life of Olbia's residents.

The rhythm of life in Olbia is both relaxed and dynamic, reflecting its dual role as a working port city and a tourist destination. Its streets are filled with the sounds of daily activity, from the chatter of locals in cafes to the hum of scooters navigating the narrow lanes. Yet, there are also moments of quiet, especially in the early morning when the city awakens to the soft light of dawn. These contrasts give Olbia a character that is both grounded and cosmopolitan, making it a place where visitors feel both connected and inspired.

As the gateway to northern Sardinia, Olbia is ideally situated for day trips and excursions. The glamour of Costa Smeralda, with its luxury resorts and idyllic beaches, is just a short drive away. The Maddalena Archipelago, a UNESCO World Heritage site, offers unparalleled opportunities for exploration, from sailing between islands to discovering hidden coves. Inland, the rugged hills and villages of Gallura reveal a different side of Sardinia, one steeped in tradition and natural beauty. Whether you're seeking adventure, relaxation, or cultural enrichment, Olbia provides the perfect starting point.

Olbia's charm lies in its ability to balance its roles as a modern hub and a repository of history and culture. It is a city that invites you to delve into its layers, from its ancient roots to its vibrant present. Whether you're savoring a meal overlooking the harbor, wandering through its historic streets, or planning your next adventure, Olbia leaves an impression that lingers long after you've departed. It is a place where the spirit of Sardinia comes alive, offering a warm welcome and endless possibilities for discovery.

Oristano: A Historic Haven

Oristano, located on Sardinia's western coast, is a city steeped in history, tradition, and understated charm. Unlike the bustling glamour of Costa Smeralda or the medieval allure of Alghero, Oristano offers a quieter, more intimate look at Sardinia's cultural and historical roots. Rich in heritage, the city is a haven for those seeking to explore Sardinia's lesser-known treasures, immersing themselves in its traditions, architecture, and the surrounding natural beauty that defines this region. Its streets, piazzas, and ancient landmarks whisper stories of a past that continues to shape the identity of this captivating city.

The city's origins can be traced back to the Middle Ages when it grew in prominence as the capital of the Giudicato of Arborea, one of the four independent kingdoms that ruled Sardinia during that period. Oristano's historical significance is best embodied by its iconic statue of Eleonora d'Arborea, a formidable figure who ruled the Giudicato in the late 14th century and is remembered as one of Sardinia's most important leaders. Her legacy endures, not only in the city's monuments but also in the Carta de Logu, the legal code she implemented, which was progressive and influential for its time. As you walk through the city, it's impossible not to feel the weight of her impact on Sardinian history.

The statue of Eleonora d'Arborea stands proudly in Piazza Eleonora, the central square that serves as the heart of Oristano. This piazza is a natural gathering place for locals and visitors alike, surrounded by historic buildings and shaded by trees that provide a tranquil respite from the midday sun. From here, the city opens up to a network of streets lined with bars, cafes, and shops, each contributing to the town's vibrant yet unhurried atmosphere. Whether you choose to linger over a coffee or explore the small artisan shops, Piazza Eleonora is the perfect starting point for discovering Oristano's unique appeal.

One of the defining landmarks in Oristano is the Tower of Mariano II, also known as the "Torre di Mariano." This imposing structure, built in the 13th century, originally formed part of the city's defensive walls. The tower stands as a testament to Oristano's medieval past, its sturdy presence a reminder of the city's strategic importance in centuries gone by. Its location at Piazza Roma makes it a focal point for visitors, and climbing to the top offers panoramic views of the city and surrounding countryside. The tower is a link to the city's historical fabric, a visual anchor that connects modern Oristano to its storied past.

The Cathedral of Santa Maria Assunta, also known as Oristano Cathedral, is another architectural gem that reflects the city's rich history. Originally constructed in the 12th century, the cathedral has undergone various transformations over the centuries, resulting in a blend of Romanesque, Gothic, and Baroque styles. Its elegant façade and towering bell tower dominate the skyline, while the interior, with its intricate altarpieces and frescoes, invites quiet contemplation. The cathedral is more than just a religious site—it is a symbol of

Oristano's enduring connection to its spiritual and cultural heritage.

Oristano's historical importance is further highlighted by its role as a center of traditional festivals and events, the most famous of which is Sa Sartiglia. This equestrian tournament, held annually during Carnival, is a spectacle unlike any other in Sardinia. Dating back to the Middle Ages, Sa Sartiglia is a celebration of chivalry, tradition, and community. Riders dressed in elaborate costumes and masks compete in a thrilling display of skill, attempting to spear a suspended star with their swords while galloping at full speed. The festival is deeply rooted in Oristano's identity, bringing the city to life with vibrant processions, music, and celebrations that draw visitors from across the island and beyond.

The city's connection to its past extends beyond its walls, with the surrounding area offering a wealth of archaeological and historical sites. One such site is the ancient city of Tharros, located on the Sinis Peninsula just a short drive from Oristano. Founded by the Phoenicians in the 8th century BCE, Tharros later became an important Carthaginian and Roman settlement. Today, its ruins provide a fascinating glimpse into the island's ancient history, with remnants of temples, baths, and a forum set against the backdrop of the Mediterranean. Wandering among the ruins, it's easy to imagine the lives of those who once called Tharros home, their stories etched into the stones that remain.

The Sinis Peninsula is also home to some of Sardinia's most stunning natural landscapes. Its unspoiled beaches, such as Is Arutas and Mari Ermi, are famous for their unique quartz sand that sparkles like tiny jewels in the sunlight. The turquoise waters of these beaches are perfect for swimming, snorkeling, or simply enjoying the serenity of this pristine environment. The peninsula's wetlands, including the Cabras Lagoon, are a haven for birdwatchers, with flamingos and other migratory species often spotted in the area. The balance between history and nature on the Sinis Peninsula makes it an essential part of any visit to Oristano.

The town of Cabras, located near Oristano, is another highlight of the region. Known for its traditional fishing culture, Cabras is famous for its bottarga, or cured mullet roe, which is a prized delicacy in Sardinian cuisine. Visitors can sample this "Mediterranean caviar" at local restaurants or purchase it from specialty shops to take home. Cabras is also the starting point for exploring the Giants of Mont'e Prama, a collection of ancient stone statues discovered in the area. These statues, thought to date back to the Nuragic civilization, are considered one of the most significant archaeological finds in Sardinia, offering a rare insight into the island's prehistoric culture.

Oristano's culinary scene is a celebration of Sardinian flavors, with an emphasis on locally sourced ingredients and traditional recipes. The region's fertile plains and proximity to the sea provide an abundance of fresh produce, seafood, and meats that form the foundation of its cuisine. Dishes such as malloreddus alla campidanese, a type of pasta served with sausage and tomato sauce, and porceddu, slow-roasted suckling pig, are staples of the local diet. Desserts like pardulas, small ricotta-filled pastries, and sebadas, a cheese-filled pastry drizzled with honey, showcase the sweet side of Sardinian gastronomy. Dining in Oristano is not just a meal but an immersion into the island's culinary traditions.

The rhythm of life in Oristano is unhurried, offering visitors a chance to slow down and appreciate the simple pleasures of Sardinian life. Its streets and squares are filled with the sounds of everyday activity, from the laughter of children playing to the chatter of locals exchanging news. Markets, such as the one held in Piazza Eleonora, provide a glimpse into the city's daily life, with stalls offering everything from fresh produce to handmade goods. Engaging with the people of Oristano, who are known for their warmth and hospitality, adds a personal dimension to the experience, leaving a lasting impression of the city's character.

Oristano's appeal lies in its ability to blend history, culture, and natural beauty into a cohesive and inviting destination. It is a city that rewards curiosity, inviting visitors to delve into its past while enjoying the tranquility of its present. Whether you're exploring its medieval landmarks, attending its vibrant festivals, or simply enjoying a leisurely meal in one of its squares, Oristano offers a unique perspective on Sardinia that is both enriching and unforgettable. It is a place where the stories of the past come alive, leaving you with a deeper appreciation for the island's heritage and the enduring spirit of its people.

Nuoro and the Heart of Sardinian Culture

Nuoro, often referred to as the cultural heart of Sardinia, offers an intimate glimpse into the island's traditions, art, and soul. Tucked into the rugged hills of central Sardinia, this small city exudes a sense of quiet pride, acting as both a guardian of the island's rich heritage and a hub for its creative and intellectual pursuits. While it may lack the coastal allure of Sardinia's beachside towns, Nuoro makes up for it with its deeply rooted traditions, fascinating history, and a connection to the Sardinian spirit that is both palpable and profound. It's a place where the past is not only preserved but celebrated, and where visitors can immerse themselves in an authentic and unvarnished experience of the island.

The city's location at the foot of Monte Ortobene enhances its distinct character. Surrounded by dramatic landscapes, Nuoro feels removed from the modernity that has touched Sardinia's more well-trodden destinations. This isolation has allowed it to retain its authenticity, making it a perfect destination for those seeking to understand the deeper layers of Sardinian identity. The mountains and rolling hills that encircle Nuoro also provide a sense of serenity, as if the city itself is cradled by the rugged beauty of its surroundings.

One of Nuoro's most celebrated figures is Grazia Deledda, a Nobel Prize-winning author whose work brought international attention to Sardinia and its culture. Deledda, who was born and raised in Nuoro, remains an enduring symbol of the city's artistic legacy. Her novels, including *Canne al Vento* (*Reeds in the Wind*), capture the essence of Sardinian life, exploring themes of tradition, morality, and the struggles of rural communities. Visitors to Nuoro can gain insight into her life and work at the Museo Deleddiano, housed in her former home. The museum is a treasure trove of personal artifacts, manuscripts, and photographs, offering a glimpse into the life of a woman who not only shaped Sardinian literature but also elevated it to the global stage.

The Museo del Costume, officially known as the Museum of Sardinian Life and Popular Traditions, is another essential stop for anyone visiting Nuoro. This museum is a vibrant celebration of Sardinia's cultural heritage, showcasing traditional clothing, jewelry, tools, and artifacts that reflect the island's diverse and ancient customs. Particularly striking are the traditional Sardinian costumes, each representing a specific region or village and adorned with intricate embroidery, vibrant colors, and unique patterns. These garments are not just pieces of clothing but symbols of identity, telling stories of the people who wore them and the communities they represented. The museum also delves into Sardinia's agricultural and pastoral traditions, offering a comprehensive look at the island's way of life over the centuries.

Nuoro's streets and squares are imbued with a sense of history and community. Piazza Sebastiano Satta, named after one of Sardinia's most beloved poets, is a focal point of the city. The square is adorned with granite sculptures created by the artist Costantino Nivola, which honor Satta's literary contributions and reflect the island's rugged landscape. This blend of art and public space creates a unique atmosphere, where poetry and sculpture intertwine, inviting visitors to pause and reflect. The square often hosts cultural events and gatherings, further emphasizing its role as a hub for Nuoro's artistic and social life.

The surrounding region, known as Barbagia, is considered the cultural heartland of Sardinia. This area, with its remote villages and timeless traditions, offers a stark contrast to the cosmopolitan atmosphere of the island's coastal cities. Barbagia is a place where ancient customs persist, from the preparation of traditional foods to the practice of age-old crafts. Villages like Orgosolo and Mamoiada, located just a short distance from Nuoro, are particularly notable for their cultural significance and their ability to transport visitors into a world that feels untouched by time.

Orgosolo is famous for its murals, which cover the walls of buildings throughout the village. These vivid works of art often depict scenes of political struggle, social commentary, and Sardinian identity, transforming the village into an open-air gallery. Strolling through Orgosolo's streets is like walking through the pages of history, with each mural offering a new perspective on the challenges and triumphs of the past and present. The murals are a testament to the resilience and creativity of the Sardinian people, encapsulating both their struggles and their pride in their heritage.

Mamoiada, on the other hand, is renowned for its ancient carnival traditions, particularly the Mamuthones and Issohadores. These traditional masked figures, dressed in dark costumes and adorned with bells, are central to the village's carnival celebrations. The Mamuthones, with their slow, rhythmic movements, and the Issohadores, with their more agile and playful demeanor, create a spectacle that is both haunting and mesmerizing. The Museum of Mediterranean Masks in Mamoiada provides further insight into these traditions, exploring the role of masks in Sardinian culture and their connections to rituals and festivals across the Mediterranean.

Nuoro's culinary offerings are deeply tied to the traditions of the Barbagia region and reflect the agricultural and pastoral roots of the area. The cuisine here is hearty and flavorful, emphasizing locally sourced ingredients and time-honored recipes. Pane carasau, a thin, crispy flatbread, is a staple of the Sardinian diet and often served with pecorino cheese or drizzled with olive oil. Culurgiones, a type of stuffed pasta resembling dumplings, are a regional specialty, filled with potato, cheese, and mint. For those with a sweet tooth, sebadas, a fried pastry filled with cheese and topped with honey, provide a delightful conclusion to any meal. Dining in Nuoro is not just about the food—it is an opportunity to connect with Sardinian traditions and the people who preserve them.

Monte Ortobene, the mountain that looms over Nuoro, is a natural landmark that holds both cultural and spiritual significance. Its slopes are dotted with walking trails that lead to breathtaking viewpoints, offering panoramic vistas of the surrounding countryside. At the summit stands the statue of Cristo Redentore (Christ the Redeemer), a symbol of faith and peace that has watched over Nuoro for more than a century. Each year, the mountain becomes the site of a religious pilgrimage and festival, drawing people from across Sardinia to celebrate and honor their shared heritage. Climbing Monte Ortobene is not just a physical journey but an emotional one, connecting visitors to the land and its traditions.

The rhythm of life in Nuoro is unhurried, allowing visitors to fully absorb the city's atmosphere and its connection to Sardinian culture. Its streets are filled with the sounds of everyday life, from the laughter of children playing in the piazzas to the melodies of traditional music drifting from a nearby café. Engaging with the people of Nuoro, who are known for their warmth and hospitality, adds a personal dimension to the experience, creating memories that linger long after you've left.

Nuoro's charm lies in its ability to celebrate Sardinia's cultural heritage while remaining firmly rooted in its present. It is a city that invites exploration, offering a wealth of experiences that capture the essence of the island's traditions, art, and way of life. Whether you're delving into its museums, savoring its cuisine, or venturing into the surrounding villages, Nuoro provides a deeper understanding of what makes Sardinia so unique. It is a place where the past and present coexist in harmony, creating a tapestry of culture and history that is as rich as it is inspiring.

Bosa: A Town of Colorful Charm

Bosa, nestled along the banks of the Temo River on Sardinia's western coast, is a town like no other. Its vibrant palette of pastel-colored houses cascading down a hill, crowned by an ancient castle, creates an image that feels almost otherworldly. A place where history, art, and natural beauty merge seamlessly, Bosa offers visitors an authentic and enchanting experience far removed from the bustling resorts of the island's more tourist-heavy regions. Strolling through its cobblestone streets, exploring its architectural gems, and soaking in its serene riverside atmosphere, you quickly realize that this is a town that holds its traditions close while embracing its whimsical charm.

The sight of Bosa from afar is nothing short of breathtaking. As you approach, the painted facades of its houses seem to glow in the Mediterranean sunlight, forming a patchwork of pinks, yellows, blues, and greens. These homes climb the slopes of Serravalle Hill, where the medieval Malaspina Castle stands watch over the town. The castle, built in the 12th century by the powerful Tuscan Malaspina family, is a reminder of Bosa's turbulent past, marked by battles for control over this strategically important location. Today, it is a symbol of resilience and history, offering panoramic views that stretch over the rooftops, the Temo River, and the surrounding countryside.

The castle itself is worth the climb, not only for its vistas but also for the treasures it holds within. Inside its walls, you'll find the small but striking Church of Nostra Signora de Sos Regnos Altos, adorned with rare medieval frescoes that depict religious scenes with an almost mystical air. These frescoes, discovered beneath layers of plaster during restoration work, are a testament to the layers of history that lie hidden within Bosa's fabric. Exploring the castle, you're transported back in time, imagining the lives of those who once sought refuge within its fortified walls.

Descending from the castle, the old town of Bosa, known as Sa Costa, invites you to wander its narrow, winding streets. These lanes, lined with colorful houses and adorned with flower-filled balconies, exude a sense of warmth and intimacy. Each turn reveals something new—a small artisan workshop, a family-run trattoria, or a hidden courtyard where locals gather to chat. The town's layout reflects its medieval origins, with irregular streets designed to confuse invaders, though today they offer nothing but delight for those who choose to get lost in their charm.

The Temo River, Sardinia's only navigable river, is the lifeblood of Bosa and a defining feature of the town. Its calm waters reflect the vibrant facades of the riverside buildings, creating a scene that feels almost like a painting. Walking along the riverbank, you'll encounter fishermen mending their nets, boats gently bobbing in the water, and the iconic Ponte Vecchio, a stone bridge that connects the two sides of the town. The river not only adds to Bosa's picturesque appeal but also plays an essential role in its history and economy, serving as a conduit for trade and a source of sustenance.

One of Bosa's most enduring traditions is the production of Malvasia di Bosa, a sweet, amber-colored wine that is as unique as the town itself. This wine, made from Malvasia grapes grown in the surrounding hills, has a distinctive flavor profile characterized by notes of honey, dried fruit, and almonds. Visiting a local cantina to sample Malvasia is an experience that connects you to the land and the generations of winemakers who have perfected their craft. Whether paired with Sardinian desserts like seadas or sipped on its own as an aperitif, Malvasia is a taste of Bosa's heritage in liquid form.

Bosa's artisanal traditions extend beyond winemaking, with the town renowned for its craftsmanship in textiles and leather goods. One of the most iconic examples is the art of filet lace, a delicate and intricate form of embroidery that has been passed down through generations. Local women still create these laceworks by hand, using techniques that require incredible skill and patience. Visiting an artisan's workshop or purchasing a piece of filet lace is not just about acquiring a beautiful item—it's about supporting a tradition that is deeply woven into the identity of Bosa.

For those interested in delving deeper into the town's history and culture, the Museo Casa Deriu provides a fascinating glimpse into Bosa's past. Housed in a 19th-century townhouse, this museum showcases period furnishings, art, and exhibits on the town's economic and social history. One section is dedicated to the work of Melkiorre Melis, a Bosa-born artist and designer who gained international acclaim for his contributions to modernist art and design. The museum captures the essence of Bosa as a place where tradition and creativity coexist, shaping a unique cultural landscape.

Nature lovers will find plenty to admire in and around Bosa, with its location offering access to both lush hills and pristine coastline. Just a short distance from the town lies Bosa Marina, a charming seaside area with a sandy beach and clear, inviting waters. The beach is ideal for swimming, sunbathing, or simply relaxing while taking in the views of the Aragonese Tower, a historic structure that stands sentinel over the coast. Further along the shoreline, the rugged cliffs and hidden coves of the Costa Verde provide opportunities for exploration and adventure, whether through hiking, snorkeling, or simply marveling at the unspoiled beauty of the landscape.

The natural environment around Bosa is also home to a remarkable array of wildlife, including one of Sardinia's most iconic species: the griffon vulture. These majestic birds, with their impressive wingspans, can often be seen soaring above the hills and cliffs near the town. The area's rich biodiversity is a testament to Sardinia's commitment to preserving its natural heritage, and witnessing these vultures in flight is a humbling reminder of the island's wild and untamed spirit.

Bosa's festivals and celebrations provide yet another layer of charm and cultural significance. One of the most notable is the Carnevale di Bosa, a lively and colorful event that showcases the town's playful side. During Carnival, the streets come alive with music, costumes, and revelry, as locals and visitors alike participate in parades and parties that reflect both Sardinian and broader Mediterranean traditions. Another highlight is the Festa di Regnos Altos, a religious festival held in honor of the Virgin Mary, featuring processions, decorations, and communal meals that bring the community together in a spirit of devotion and celebration.

The rhythm of life in Bosa is unhurried, allowing visitors to fully immerse themselves in its atmosphere and appreciate the small details that make it so special. Whether it's the sound of church bells echoing through the streets, the aroma of freshly baked bread wafting from a bakery, or the sight of children playing along the riverbank, every moment feels like an invitation to slow down and savor the simple pleasures of this enchanting town.

Bosa's magic lies in its ability to be both timeless and vibrant, a place where history and tradition are not merely preserved but actively celebrated. It is a town that invites you to explore, to connect, and to be inspired by its beauty and authenticity. Whether you're gazing at its colorful houses from the castle, sipping Malvasia by the river, or simply wandering its cobblestone streets, Bosa leaves an impression that lingers long after you've departed. It is not just a destination but an experience, a reminder of the enduring charm and character of Sardinia's hidden gems.

La Maddalena Archipelago: Island-Hopping Bliss

The La Maddalena Archipelago, a cluster of islands scattered like emeralds in the turquoise waters off Sardinia's northeastern coast, is a paradise that promises an unforgettable experience for those who venture to its shores. Comprising seven larger islands and an array of smaller islets, this protected national park is a sanctuary of unspoiled beauty, marine biodiversity, and historical intrigue. While well-known among seasoned Mediterranean travelers, the archipelago retains an air of exclusivity, offering pristine beaches, secluded coves, and crystal-clear waters that rival any tropical destination. From the moment you set foot on its islands, you'll understand why La Maddalena is considered one of Sardinia's most treasured gems.

The journey to La Maddalena begins with a short ferry ride from the mainland town of Palau, a gateway to the archipelago. As the ferry glides across the water, you're greeted by views of rugged coastlines, shimmering seas, and distant islands that appear to float on the horizon. This brief crossing serves as an introduction to the archipelago's natural splendor, heightening the anticipation of what lies ahead. The main island, also called La Maddalena, is the first stop for most visitors, and its charming town is the beating heart of the archipelago.

The town of La Maddalena is a delightful blend of old-world charm and Mediterranean vibrancy. Its narrow streets, lined with pastel-colored buildings and bustling with local life, invite exploration. The central Piazza Garibaldi, named after the legendary Italian general who played a significant role in unifying Italy, is a focal point where locals and visitors gather to enjoy the laid-back atmosphere. Cafes spill out onto the square, offering the perfect spot to sip an espresso or indulge in Sardinian pastries while watching the world go by. The town's harbor is equally captivating, with fishing boats and yachts swaying gently in the breeze, creating a scene that epitomizes coastal allure.

While the town offers a taste of island life, the real magic of La Maddalena lies in its natural landscapes and surrounding waters. The main island is crisscrossed with scenic roads and hiking trails that lead to breathtaking viewpoints and hidden beaches. One of the most popular routes is the panoramic road known as Strada Panoramica, which encircles the island and offers spectacular views of the archipelago and the nearby Corsican coast. Along the way, you'll encounter coves and beaches where you can pause for a swim or simply take in the beauty of your surroundings.

Among the many beaches on La Maddalena, Spiaggia di Bassa Trinità stands out for its fine white sand and calm, inviting waters. This beach, like many in the archipelago, feels untouched by time, offering a sense of serenity that is increasingly rare in today's world. For those seeking a more secluded experience, the smaller coves tucked along the coastline provide an opportunity to escape the crowds and immerse yourself in nature's tranquility. Each beach has its own character, from the rugged charm of Cala Francese to the shallow, family-friendly waters of Cala Spalmatore.

Exploring the archipelago's other islands is an essential part of the La Maddalena experience, and boat tours or private charters are the best way to navigate these pristine waters. The island of Caprera, connected to La Maddalena by a narrow causeway, is a favorite among visitors for its wild beauty and historical significance. Caprera is home to the Garibaldi Compendium, a museum and memorial dedicated to Giuseppe Garibaldi, who spent the last years of his life on the island. His house, preserved as it was during his lifetime, offers a fascinating glimpse into the life of one of Italy's most revered figures. Walking through its rooms and gardens, you can feel the weight of history that permeates this tranquil corner of the archipelago.

Caprera is equally renowned for its beaches, including Spiaggia del Relitto, named for the remnants of a shipwreck that lie just offshore. Its shallow, crystalline waters and soft sand create a picture-perfect setting that feels almost untouched by human hands. Cala Coticcio, often referred to as "Tahiti" for its striking resemblance to Polynesian lagoons, is another highlight. Accessible via a scenic hike or by boat, this cove is a paradise for snorkeling and swimming, with its vibrant marine life and luminous blue waters.

Further afield, the islands of Spargi, Budelli, and Razzoli beckon with their own unique charms. Spargi, with its dramatic cliffs and hidden bays, is a haven for adventurers and nature lovers. Cala Corsara, one of its most famous beaches, is framed by sculpted granite rocks that seem to defy gravity. Budelli, perhaps the most iconic of the archipelago's islands, is renowned for its Spiaggia Rosa, or Pink Beach. The sand here owes its distinctive hue to microscopic fragments of coral and shells, creating a phenomenon that has captivated visitors for decades. While the beach itself is now protected and off-limits to the public to preserve its delicate ecosystem, its beauty can still be admired from afar.

The archipelago's marine environment is as extraordinary as its landscapes, making it a paradise for snorkeling and diving enthusiasts. The waters surrounding La Maddalena are teeming with life, from colorful fish and octopuses to seagrass meadows that provide a vital habitat for marine species. Diving excursions reveal underwater caves, shipwrecks, and coral formations that rival the beauty of the islands above. The area's status as a national park ensures that these ecosystems are carefully preserved, offering a chance to experience the Mediterranean at its most pristine.

History buffs will find plenty to explore in La Maddalena beyond its natural wonders. The archipelago's strategic location has made it a crossroads of maritime activity for centuries, from ancient seafarers to naval fleets. Fortifications and ruins scattered across the islands tell stories of battles and alliances, while the Naval Museum in the town of La Maddalena provides insight into the region's maritime heritage. The museum's exhibits, which include artifacts from the Napoleonic Wars and World War II, offer a deeper understanding of the archipelago's role in shaping Mediterranean history.

For those seeking a more active adventure, the archipelago offers opportunities for kayaking, paddleboarding, and sailing. Gliding across the azure waters, you'll discover hidden caves and secluded coves that are inaccessible by land. The gentle sea breeze and warm sun create ideal conditions for these activities, allowing you to connect with the natural beauty of La Maddalena in an intimate and exhilarating way.

Food and drink are integral to the La Maddalena experience, with the islands' cuisine reflecting Sardinia's rich culinary traditions. Fresh seafood takes center stage, from grilled fish and octopus to spaghetti with sea urchin. Local delicacies such as bottarga, a cured fish roe often referred to as "Sardinian caviar," add a touch of indulgence to any meal. Pairing these dishes with a glass of Vermentino di Gallura, a crisp white wine produced in the nearby Gallura region, enhances the flavors and provides a true taste of the Mediterranean.

Evenings in La Maddalena are a time for relaxation and reflection. As the sun sets over the archipelago, the town's streets come alive with the hum of conversation and the clinking of glasses. Whether dining al fresco at a waterfront trattoria, strolling along the harbor, or simply sitting by the water's edge, the magic of the islands is undeniable. The gentle lapping of waves and the warm glow of lanterns create an atmosphere that is both romantic and serene.

The La Maddalena Archipelago is more than just a destination—it is an invitation to slow down, to connect with nature, and to immerse yourself in the timeless beauty of Sardinia's northern coast. Whether you're exploring its historic town, swimming in its crystalline waters, or marveling at its untouched landscapes, the archipelago offers a sense of wonder that stays with you long after you leave. It is a place where the rhythm of the sea sets the pace of life, and where every moment feels like a gift.

Barbagia: Sardinia's Rugged Interior

Barbagia, the rugged and unyielding heart of Sardinia, is a land where traditions run deep, landscapes remain untamed, and Sardinian identity is fiercely preserved. Nestled in the mountainous interior of the island, this region is a stark contrast to the turquoise beaches and luxury resorts that define Sardinia's coastal allure. Instead, Barbagia offers a raw and unfiltered glimpse into the soul of the island, where ancient customs, hearty cuisine, and a proud, independent spirit still thrive. It is a place where visitors can step off the beaten path and discover a side of Sardinia that is as authentic as it is captivating.

The region's name, derived from the Latin *Barbaria*, reflects the Roman view of the area as wild and unconquered. While much of Sardinia fell under Roman rule, Barbagia's rugged terrain and defiant inhabitants made it a bastion of resistance.

This spirit of independence remains woven into the fabric of Barbagia's identity, evident in the way its people have held onto their traditions and way of life over the centuries. The villages scattered across the region are living testaments to this resilience, where ancient practices are not relics of the past but integral parts of daily life.

At the heart of Barbagia lies the imposing Gennargentu mountain range, Sardinia's highest peaks. These mountains dominate the landscape, their jagged summits often shrouded in mist, lending an air of mystery to the region. Hiking through Gennargentu reveals breathtaking vistas, from rolling hills carpeted in wildflowers to deep valleys carved by rivers and streams. The area is a haven for nature enthusiasts, offering trails that range from leisurely walks to challenging ascents. Along the way, you might encounter shepherds tending their flocks, a reminder of the region's enduring connection to its pastoral roots.

One of the most enchanting villages in Barbagia is Orgosolo, renowned for its vibrant murals that adorn nearly every building. These murals, or *murales*, began as a form of protest art in the mid-20th century, addressing political and social issues both local and global. Over time, the tradition has evolved, and today the murals reflect a wide range of themes, from Sardinian folklore to contemporary struggles for justice and equality. Walking through Orgosolo is like exploring an open-air gallery, each mural telling a story that adds to the rich tapestry of the village's identity.

Mamoiada, another gem of Barbagia, is famous for its ancient carnival traditions. The Mamuthones and Issohadores, the masked figures central to these celebrations, are among Sardinia's most iconic symbols. The Mamuthones, clad in black sheepskins and heavy cowbells, move in slow, deliberate steps, embodying a sense of solemnity and mystery. In contrast, the Issohadores, dressed in white and red, dance with agility and energy, casting ropes to "capture" bystanders in a playful gesture. This contrast between the two figures creates a dynamic and mesmerizing performance that has been passed down through generations. The Museum of Mediterranean Masks in Mamoiada provides deeper insight into these traditions, exploring their origins and significance.

Barbagia's culinary traditions are as robust and unpretentious as the region itself. The cuisine here is deeply rooted in the land, with dishes that highlight local ingredients and time-honored techniques. Pane carasau, a thin, crispy flatbread, is a staple of the Sardinian diet and a product of Barbagia's pastoral heritage. Known as "shepherd's bread," it was designed to last for weeks, making it ideal for those who spent long periods in the mountains. Su porcheddu, or roast suckling pig, is another iconic dish, prepared with a simplicity that allows the natural flavors of the meat to shine. It is often cooked over an open fire and seasoned with little more than salt, myrtle, and rosemary.

Cheese plays a central role in the region's gastronomy, with pecorino and ricotta being among the most celebrated varieties. These cheeses, made from sheep's milk, reflect the region's pastoral economy and are often enjoyed with a drizzle of Sardinian honey or paired with a glass of Cannonau wine. Cannonau, a robust red wine believed to be one of the oldest grape varieties in the Mediterranean, is the perfect accompaniment to Barbagia's hearty fare. Its bold flavors and rich history embody the spirit of the region, making it a must-try for any visitor.

History enthusiasts will find much to explore in Barbagia, from its Nuragic sites to its medieval churches. The Nuragic civilization, which flourished in Sardinia between 1800 and 500 BCE, left behind a remarkable legacy of stone towers, villages, and tombs. One of the most significant sites in Barbagia is the Nuraghe Losa, an impressive complex that offers a glimpse into the island's prehistoric past. Walking among its massive basalt stones, you can't help but marvel at the ingenuity and resilience of Sardinia's ancient inhabitants.

The region's connection to its history is also evident in its festivals and rituals, many of which have roots in pre-Christian traditions. The *Ardia di San Costantino*, held in the village of Sedilo, is a thrilling horse race that combines religious devotion with ancient customs. Riders, dressed in traditional attire, race through the streets at breakneck speeds, their movements a blend of skill, courage, and reverence. The festival is as much a celebration of community as it is a display of horsemanship, drawing spectators from across Sardinia and beyond.

Barbagia's landscapes are as diverse as they are breathtaking. The Supramonte plateau, with its limestone cliffs, caves, and canyons, is a haven for adventurers. Gorropu Gorge, often referred to as Europe's Grand Canyon, is one of the region's most spectacular natural wonders. Its towering walls, which reach heights of over 500 meters, create a dramatic backdrop for hiking and climbing. Exploring Gorropu is an awe-inspiring experience, offering a sense of scale and wonder that is difficult to put into words.

For those seeking a more tranquil connection with nature, the region's forests and woodlands provide a serene escape. The holm oak and cork oak forests that blanket the hills are home to a variety of wildlife, from wild boar and deer to golden eagles and Sardinian foxes. These natural habitats are a reminder of Barbagia's wild and untamed character, a place where nature remains unspoiled and life moves at its own pace.

The people of Barbagia, known for their hospitality and pride in their heritage, are an integral part of the region's appeal. Engaging with the locals, whether over a shared meal or during a village festival, provides a deeper understanding of what makes Barbagia so special. Their stories, traditions, and way of life offer a window into a Sardinia that is both timeless and unique.

Barbagia is not a place to be rushed. Its beauty lies in its depth, its ability to reveal itself slowly to those who take the time to look beyond the surface. From its ancient sites and dramatic landscapes to its vibrant festivals and rich culinary traditions, this is a region that rewards curiosity and invites exploration. It is a place where the past and present coexist in harmony, creating a tapestry of culture and history that is as complex as it is captivating. For those willing to venture into Sardinia's rugged interior, Barbagia offers an experience that is both enriching and unforgettable.

CHAPTER 3: STUNNING BEACHES AND COASTAL ESCAPES

The Most Iconic Beaches: Cala Luna, Cala Goloritzé, and Spiaggia del Principe

Cala Luna, Cala Goloritzé, and Spiaggia del Principe represent some of Sardinia's most iconic beaches, each offering a unique combination of natural beauty, pristine waters, and unforgettable experiences. These stunning locations are more than just places to relax by the sea—they are destinations that evoke a deeper connection to Sardinia's extraordinary landscape. From dramatic cliffs and hidden caves to powdery sands and turquoise waters, these beaches are the epitome of the island's allure. Their fame is well-deserved, yet they remain unspoiled havens where nature takes center stage. Visiting these beaches is not merely about swimming or sunbathing; it is about immersing yourself in some of the most breathtaking scenery the Mediterranean has to offer.

Cala Luna, located along the eastern coast near the Gulf of Orosei, is a dazzling crescent of golden sand framed by imposing limestone cliffs and lush greenery. Its name, which translates to "Moon Cove," captures something of its otherworldly beauty. Accessible by boat or a challenging hike through the rugged Supramonte mountains, reaching Cala Luna feels like a rewarding adventure in itself. The journey through the dense Mediterranean maquis, with its aromatic shrubs and wildflowers, opens up to a view that takes your breath away. The beach stretches for nearly 700 meters, offering plenty of space to find your own slice of paradise.

The most striking feature of Cala Luna is its dramatic juxtaposition of land and sea. The cliffs that envelop the cove are punctuated by large caves, some of which open directly onto the beach. These caves provide natural shade and a touch of mystery, inviting exploration or simply offering a cool retreat from the midday sun. Their smooth, weathered interiors speak to centuries of erosion by wind and waves, creating a timeless ambiance that enhances the beach's allure. For those with a sense of adventure, the combination of climbing and snorkeling opportunities around the cliffs and caves adds an extra layer of excitement to a visit.

The waters of Cala Luna are an irresistible shade of blue, transitioning from aquamarine near the shore to deeper hues farther out. The clarity of the sea makes it an ideal spot for snorkeling, where you can observe schools of fish darting among submerged rock formations. The shallow areas near the beach are perfect for families with young children, while the deeper sections farther out are a haven for more experienced swimmers. Whether you are paddling in the gentle waves or diving into the crystalline depths, the experience is one of pure tranquility.

Cala Goloritzé, often regarded as one of Sardinia's most iconic natural wonders, is a beach that defies expectations. Declared a UNESCO World Heritage Site, it is a protected gem that exemplifies the island's commitment to preserving its natural beauty. Located further south along the Gulf of Orosei, Cala Goloritzé is not accessible by boat, ensuring it remains a serene and unspoiled destination. Instead, visitors must trek through a two-hour hiking trail that begins in the village of Baunei. The journey, while demanding, is part of what makes Cala Goloritzé so special. Each step through the rocky terrain and shaded groves feels like a pilgrimage to a sacred site, heightening the anticipation of what awaits.

Arriving at Cala Goloritzé is a moment of awe. The beach is small yet perfectly formed, with smooth white pebbles that gleam in the sunlight and waters so clear they seem almost unreal. The iconic limestone pinnacle known as Aguglia di Goloritzé rises 143 meters above the cove, creating a dramatic backdrop that has made the beach a favorite among climbers. This towering spire is not just a geological marvel but also a symbol of the untamed beauty of Sardinia's interior meeting the sea. The contrast between the rugged cliffs and the gentle lapping of the waves creates a sense of harmony that is difficult to describe.

The underwater world of Cala Goloritzé is equally captivating. Snorkeling here reveals a vibrant marine ecosystem, with colorful fish darting through seagrass meadows and rocky crevices. The purity of the waters, fed by freshwater springs that bubble up from the seabed, adds to the beach's magical quality. Swimming in these waters feels almost like floating in a natural pool, surrounded by a setting so pristine it seems untouched by time. The absence of commercial facilities or crowds further enhances the sense of being in a hidden paradise, making every moment at Cala Goloritzé feel like a rare privilege.

Spiaggia del Principe, located on the northern coast near the glamorous Costa Smeralda, offers a different yet equally enchanting beach experience. Its name, which translates to "The Prince's Beach," is said to derive from Prince Karim Aga Khan, the founder of Costa Smeralda, who reportedly declared it his favorite spot on the island. It is easy to see why. Spiaggia del Principe is a picture-perfect arc of soft white sand lapped by waters that shimmer in varying shades of blue and green. Enclosed by granite rocks that form natural barriers, the beach exudes an air of exclusivity while remaining welcoming to all who venture there.

Unlike Cala Luna or Cala Goloritzé, Spiaggia del Principe is easily accessible, with a short walk from a nearby parking area. Despite its proximity to the luxury resorts of Costa Smeralda, the beach retains a low-key charm that makes it feel more authentic than commercialized. The surrounding landscape, with its rugged rocks and fragrant juniper trees, adds to the sense of being in a secluded oasis. The beach's shallow waters and gentle waves make it ideal for families and less experienced swimmers, while its calm conditions are perfect for paddleboarding or simply floating on the surface.

What sets Spiaggia del Principe apart is the quality of its sand and water. The sand, fine and powdery, feels like silk beneath your feet, while the water is so transparent that you can see every ripple and pebble on the seabed. The interplay of light and color creates a mesmerizing effect, with the water appearing to glow in hues of turquoise, emerald, and sapphire. This optical phenomenon, caused by the unique mineral composition of the sand and rocks, has made Spiaggia del Principe a favorite subject for photographers and painters seeking to capture its ethereal beauty.

Each of these beaches offers something unique, yet they all share the qualities that make Sardinia one of the most sought-after destinations in the Mediterranean. Cala Luna enchants with its caves and adventurous spirit, Cala Goloritzé captivates with its pristine isolation and dramatic cliffs, and Spiaggia del Principe delights with its effortless elegance and vibrant colors. Together, they showcase the diversity and splendor of

Sardinia's coastline, inviting visitors to explore, relax, and reconnect with nature.

Visiting these iconic beaches is not just about enjoying their beauty but also about respecting and preserving their natural environments. The efforts to protect these sites, from regulating access to limiting human impact, ensure that future generations can experience their magic. Whether you arrive by boat, hike through mountain trails, or simply stroll from a nearby path, the journey to these beaches is as memorable as the destination itself. Sardinia's coastline is a reminder of the power and serenity of nature, and these beaches are its crowning jewels.

Hidden Beaches and Secluded Coves

Hidden beaches and secluded coves are Sardinia's best-kept secrets, scattered along its rugged coastline and waiting to be discovered by those willing to venture off the beaten path. These remote spots offer an escape from the crowds, providing a sense of solitude and intimacy that is increasingly rare in today's world. Tucked away behind cliffs, dense Mediterranean vegetation, or accessible only by boat, these hidden gems reward the adventurous with unspoiled beauty and an unmatched connection to nature. They are places where time seems to stand still, and the only sounds are the gentle lapping of waves and the rustle of the wind through the rocks and trees.

One such treasure is Cala Domestica, located on the southwestern coast of Sardinia, near the former mining town of Buggerru. Framed by towering limestone cliffs, this small, sheltered beach is a tranquil oasis that feels like a world apart.

Cala Domestica's golden sands extend gently into crystal-clear waters, creating the perfect setting for swimming or simply basking in the sun. What makes this beach particularly special is the hidden cove that lies just beyond it. Accessible through a natural tunnel carved into the rock, the cove offers an even greater sense of seclusion, with its own tiny stretch of sand and a feeling of total privacy. Exploring this secret spot is like uncovering a piece of paradise, a memory that stays with you long after you leave.

On the eastern coast, Cala Fuili is another stunning example of Sardinia's secluded beaches. Situated near the town of Cala Gonone, Cala Fuili is the last beach accessible by road before the coastline becomes a series of remote coves reachable only by foot or boat. To reach Cala Fuili, visitors must descend a series of stone steps that wind their way down the cliffside, offering breathtaking views of the turquoise sea below. The descent itself feels like an adventure, heightening the anticipation of what awaits. Once you arrive, you're greeted by a pebble beach surrounded by rugged cliffs and dense vegetation. The waters here are exceptionally clear, revealing a vibrant underwater world that makes snorkeling an absolute must. Cala Fuili's relative inaccessibility ensures it remains uncrowded, allowing visitors to enjoy its natural beauty in peace.

Further south along the eastern coast lies Cala Biriola, a true hidden gem that embodies the wild and untamed spirit of Sardinia. Accessible only by boat or via a challenging hiking trail through the forested Supramonte plateau, Cala Biriola is the very definition of a secluded cove. Its small pebble beach is framed by steep cliffs covered in juniper and holm oak trees, creating a natural amphitheater that feels both intimate and majestic. The sea here is a kaleidoscope of blues and greens, so clear that you can see the seabed even in the deeper sections. Cala Biriola is also known for its unique underwater rock formations, making it a favorite among divers and snorkelers. Exploring these formations, you'll encounter schools of fish, vibrant coral, and perhaps even the occasional octopus, all thriving in this pristine marine environment.

On the opposite side of the island, the Costa Verde, or "Green Coast," offers a completely different yet equally enchanting experience. This remote stretch of coastline is characterized by its wild, windswept beauty, with dunes, rocky outcrops, and beaches that seem to stretch endlessly into the horizon. One of the most secluded spots here is Spiaggia di Scivu, a vast expanse of golden sand backed by rolling dunes and cliffs. The beach's remote location and lack of development make it a haven for those seeking solitude and a connection to nature. Walking along the shore, you'll often find yourself completely alone, with only the sound of the waves and the cry of seabirds to accompany you. Spiaggia di Scivu's untamed beauty is a reminder of Sardinia's raw and unspoiled essence.

Another hidden gem on the Costa Verde is Cala Sapone, located on the island of Sant'Antioco, just off Sardinia's southwestern coast. Unlike many of the island's more famous beaches, Cala Sapone is best known for its rocky shoreline, which creates a series of natural pools and inlets perfect for swimming and exploring. The rocks are smooth and flat, making them ideal for sunbathing, while the pools are teeming with marine life, offering endless opportunities for snorkeling. Cala Sapone's remote location ensures a tranquil atmosphere, and its dramatic sunsets, with the sun dipping below the horizon in a blaze of orange and pink, are nothing short of magical.

For those willing to venture even further off the beaten path, the island of Asinara in the far north of Sardinia offers some of the most secluded beaches in the region. Once a penal colony and now a protected national park, Asinara is a place where nature reigns supreme. Access to the island is strictly regulated, with only a limited number of visitors allowed each day, ensuring its pristine environment remains untouched. Cala Sabina, one of Asinara's most beautiful beaches, is a secluded cove of white sand and azure waters surrounded by rugged hills. Reaching Cala Sabina requires a hike through the island's arid landscape, but the effort is more than worth it. The beach's isolation and untouched beauty make it feel like a secret known only to a lucky few.

Another highlight of Asinara is Cala d'Arena, often regarded as one of the most beautiful beaches in Sardinia. Completely off-limits to visitors to protect its delicate ecosystem, Cala d'Arena can only be admired from a distance, adding to its mystique. The beach's pristine sand and dazzling waters are a testament to the island's commitment to conservation, preserving its natural heritage for future generations. While you may not be able to set foot on Cala d'Arena, simply witnessing its untouched beauty is an experience in itself, a reminder of the importance of protecting Sardinia's hidden treasures.

The allure of these hidden beaches and secluded coves lies not only in their beauty but also in the sense of discovery they inspire. Each one offers a unique experience, from the adventurous hikes required to reach Cala Goloritzé to the tranquil pools of Cala Sapone and the windswept expanses of Spiaggia di Scivu. They are places where you can leave the world behind and lose yourself in the rhythm of the sea, the warmth of the sun, and the timeless beauty of Sardinia's coastline. Exploring these secret spots is not just about finding a place to relax—it's about connecting with the island's wild spirit and creating memories that will linger long after the journey ends. Sardinia's hidden beaches and coves are more than just destinations; they are invitations to explore, to dream, and to experience the magic of nature in its purest form.

Activities for Beach Lovers: Snorkeling, Diving, and Windsurfing

Sardinia's crystal-clear waters and diverse coastline make it a playground for beach lovers, offering an incredible array of activities that go far beyond lounging in the sun. For those who crave adventure and an intimate connection with the sea, snorkeling, diving, and windsurfing are some of the most rewarding ways to explore the island's aquatic wonders. These activities not only immerse you in Sardinia's spectacular marine environment but also provide an opportunity to engage with the island's landscapes in a way that feels both exhilarating and deeply personal. Whether you're plunging into the depths of the Mediterranean, gliding across its surface, or marveling at its underwater life, Sardinia's beaches offer something for every kind of sea enthusiast.

Snorkeling in Sardinia is like entering a magical underwater world, where vibrant marine life and stunning seascapes come alive beneath the surface. The island's waters are renowned for their remarkable clarity, often providing visibility of up to 30 meters, which allows snorkelers to fully appreciate the beauty that lies below. One of the best places to snorkel is the La Maddalena Archipelago, a protected marine park in the north. The shallow reefs and rocky outcrops around islands such as Spargi and Budelli are teeming with life. Here, you can expect to encounter schools of colorful fish, starfish clinging to rocks, and even curious octopuses weaving their way through seagrass meadows. The Pink Beach of Budelli, though off-limits to visitors to protect its delicate environment, remains a breathtaking sight from the water, and the surrounding areas provide plenty of snorkeling opportunities.

On the eastern coast, the Gulf of Orosei offers some of the most dramatic snorkeling spots. Cala Mariolu, with its pebble beach and dazzlingly clear waters, is a favorite among both locals and visitors. The underwater scenery here is mesmerizing, featuring intricate rock formations, tunnels, and caves that are perfect for exploration. Swimming alongside shoals of damselfish or catching a glimpse of a moray eel peeking out from a crevice adds a thrill to the experience. The calm and sheltered conditions of Cala Mariolu make it ideal for beginners, while more experienced snorkelers can venture further out to discover hidden treasures beneath the waves.

For a completely different snorkeling experience, the southwestern coast offers the unique marine environment of Sant'Antioco and Carloforte. These areas, known for their volcanic rock formations and rich biodiversity, are a haven for those looking to explore less crowded waters. The rocky seabed around Cala Sapone on Sant'Antioco creates a fascinating underwater landscape, with natural pools and crevices that attract a variety of marine species. Carloforte, on the island of San Pietro, is famous for its tuna fishing heritage, and snorkeling here offers the chance to see larger fish as well as vibrant smaller species that thrive in its nutrient-rich waters.

For those seeking a more immersive underwater adventure, diving in Sardinia opens up an entirely new realm of exploration. The island's coastline is dotted with dive sites that cater to all levels of experience, from shallow reefs ideal for beginners to deep wrecks and caves that challenge even the most seasoned divers. One of the most famous dive sites in Sardinia is the Grotta del Nereo, located near Alghero on the island's northwestern coast. Often referred to as the "Mediterranean's largest underwater cave," this site is a labyrinth of tunnels and chambers filled with stunning rock formations, stalactites, and stalagmites. The entrance to the cave, set at a depth of around 30 meters, is surrounded by an abundance of marine life, including groupers, barracudas, and vibrant nudibranchs. Exploring the Grotta del Nereo is an unforgettable experience that combines natural beauty with the thrill of discovery.

Wreck diving enthusiasts will find Sardinia equally rewarding, with numerous sunken ships and planes that tell stories of the region's history. Off the coast of Cagliari in the south, the wreck of the Romagna, a cargo ship that sank during World War II, lies at a depth of around 30 meters. The ship is now an artificial reef, home to an array of marine life that has taken up residence among its rusting hull and decks. Divers can explore the remains of the ship while encountering octopuses, sea bream, and even the occasional dolphin that passes through the area. Further north, near the island of Tavolara, lies another famous wreck, the KT12, a German cargo ship sunk in 1943. The wreck is surrounded by shoals of fish and covered in colorful coral, making it a fascinating dive for those interested in both history and marine ecosystems.

Cave diving is another highlight of Sardinia's underwater offerings. The island's limestone coastline is riddled with caves and grottoes, many of which are accessible only by diving. The Blue Cave near Cala Gonone is a particularly striking example, with its vivid blue waters illuminated by sunlight filtering through an underwater entrance. Diving into this otherworldly environment feels almost surreal, as if you've entered a hidden paradise. The Cave of Fico, near Baunei, is another must-visit site, known for its impressive stalactites and stalagmites as well as the possibility of encountering monk seals, a critically endangered species that occasionally inhabits the area.

For those who prefer to stay above the water but still crave adventure, windsurfing in Sardinia provides an exhilarating way to experience the island's coastal beauty. With its consistent winds and diverse range of conditions, Sardinia is considered one of the best windsurfing destinations in the Mediterranean. The northern region of Porto Pollo, near Palau, is a mecca for windsurfing enthusiasts, drawing both beginners and professionals from around the world. The area is known for its steady Mistral winds, which create ideal conditions for gliding across the water. The bay is divided into two sections, one catering to beginners with calmer waters and the other offering more challenging waves for experienced windsurfers.

In the south, the beaches of Poetto and Chia are popular windsurfing spots that combine excellent conditions with stunning scenery. Poetto, near the capital city of Cagliari, offers long stretches of sandy beach and reliable thermal winds, making it a great place for beginners to learn the basics. Chia, with its turquoise waters and dramatic dunes, provides a more picturesque setting and is particularly favored during the spring and autumn months when the winds are at their best. Both locations offer windsurfing schools and equipment rentals, ensuring that even newcomers can join in the fun.

For a truly unique windsurfing experience, the island of Sant'Antioco offers a blend of challenging conditions and unspoiled landscapes. The windswept coastline here creates the perfect environment for advanced windsurfers, with strong gusts and rolling waves that test both skill and endurance. The sense of freedom that comes from skimming across the water, with the rugged beauty of Sardinia as your backdrop, is unmatched, making every session an unforgettable adventure.

What makes Sardinia so special for beach lovers is the sheer variety of experiences it offers. Snorkeling, diving, and windsurfing each provide a different perspective on the island's natural beauty, allowing you to engage with its marine environment in ways that are as thrilling as they are memorable. Whether you're discovering hidden underwater caves, gliding across turquoise waves, or marveling at the vibrant life beneath the surface, Sardinia invites you to immerse yourself fully in its extraordinary world. These activities are not just about recreation—they are about forging a deeper connection with the sea, the land, and the timeless spirit of this remarkable island.

Family-Friendly Beaches

Sardinia's coastline stretches for nearly 2,000 kilometers and offers an incredible variety of beaches, many of which are perfectly suited for families seeking safe, relaxing, and enjoyable seaside experiences. Family-friendly beaches in Sardinia stand out not only for their calm, shallow waters and soft sands but also for the ease of access, available amenities, and the sense of security they provide for parents and children alike. These beaches allow families to create lasting memories, whether building sandcastles, splashing in crystal-clear waters, or exploring the natural surroundings. Sardinia, with its natural beauty and family-oriented atmosphere, provides a perfect destination for all ages.

On the northeastern coast, La Cinta Beach in San Teodoro is a quintessential family favorite. Its vast expanse of powdery white sand stretches for several kilometers, providing plenty of space for children to run and play freely. The shallow waters extend far from the shore, allowing even the youngest swimmers to wade safely while parents relax nearby. The gentle slope of the seabed ensures calm conditions, making it ideal for families with toddlers or less confident swimmers. Beyond the beach itself, La Cinta is well-equipped with facilities, including beach bars, restrooms, and sunbed rentals, ensuring convenience for families. Close to the beach, the lagoon of San Teodoro offers an exciting opportunity to spot flamingos and other bird species, adding a touch of nature exploration to the day.

Another gem for families is Porto Giunco in Villasimius, located on the southeastern coast. This beach combines breathtaking beauty with family-friendly features, creating an idyllic setting for a day by the sea. The sand is soft and golden, and the waters are calm and inviting, with a stunning turquoise hue that mesmerizes visitors of all ages. Porto Giunco is particularly well-suited for families because of its long, shallow shoreline, which allows children to play safely in the water. The surrounding area offers shaded spots under pine trees and plenty of parking, making it easy to spend an entire day here without hassle. For older children, kayaking or paddleboarding in the tranquil waters provides a fun and active way to explore the coastline.

In the north, Porto Istana stands out as a peaceful haven for families. Located near Olbia, this beach is a series of small coves separated by rocky outcrops, offering a sense of privacy and calm. The sand is fine and soft, perfect for little ones to dig and build castles, while the shallow waters are crystal clear, making it easy for parents to keep an eye on their children. The beach is also sheltered from strong winds, ensuring a tranquil environment even on breezier days. Nearby, families can find picnic spots and small kiosks offering snacks and refreshments, making Porto Istana as practical as it is picturesque.

The southwestern coast brings its own charm with the beach of Porto Pino, known for its striking white dunes and tranquil waters. This beach is a favorite among families due to its size and versatility. The gentle slope of the seabed makes it safe for young swimmers, while older children can explore the dunes or paddle along the shore. Porto Pino's relatively remote location means it is less crowded than some of the island's more famous beaches, providing a peaceful retreat for families seeking a more relaxed atmosphere. The nearby lagoon is also home to flamingos, adding an element of wildlife discovery to the visit.

Families visiting the Costa Rei in the southeastern part of the island will find a wide range of beaches that cater to every need. One of the highlights is Cala Sinzias, a serene stretch of sand surrounded by lush greenery and gentle hills. The beach's calm waters and clean, well-maintained environment make it a top choice for families. Amenities such as parking, beach bars, and restaurants are easily accessible, and the area's natural beauty creates a tranquil backdrop for a day of fun and relaxation. For parents seeking a balance of leisure and activity, Cala Sinzias also offers opportunities for snorkeling and boat trips, ensuring everyone in the family can enjoy their time to the fullest.

Southwest of Cagliari, the beach of Nora provides an exceptional combination of relaxation and cultural enrichment for families. While the beach itself features shallow waters and soft sand ideal for children, it is also located near the archaeological site of Nora, one of Sardinia's most important Roman ruins. Families can spend the morning exploring ancient mosaics, baths, and amphitheaters before heading to the beach for an afternoon of swimming and unwinding. The dual experience of history and leisure makes Nora a unique destination that appeals to both children and adults.

On the western coast, the beach of Is Arutas offers a fascinating experience with its distinctive quartz sand. The tiny, multicolored grains of quartz create a dazzling effect, and the texture is soft and cool underfoot, making it a novelty for children to discover. While the waters here can be slightly deeper than those of other family-friendly beaches, the calm conditions on most days ensure a safe environment for swimming. Families can bring umbrellas or rent them on-site to enjoy a comfortable day in this unique setting. The surrounding area also offers smaller coves and picnic areas, providing a change of scenery and additional activities for families to enjoy.

For those in search of a more intimate atmosphere, Cala Brandinchi, often referred to as "Little Tahiti," is a must-visit. This beach, located near San Teodoro, features fine white sand and shallow, turquoise waters that seem to glow in the sunlight. The beach's calm conditions make it perfect for children, while the lush vegetation surrounding the area provides shade and a sense of seclusion. Cala Brandinchi is also an excellent spot for snorkeling, with its clear waters revealing schools of fish and interesting underwater features. The nearby amenities, including parking, food vendors, and restrooms, ensure a stress-free experience for families.

In the far south, Tuerredda Beach is another standout destination for families. Nestled between Capo Malfatano and Capo Spartivento, this beach is often regarded as one of Sardinia's most beautiful. The crescent-shaped bay is protected from strong winds, and the shallow waters are warm and inviting, perfect for young children. The beach's striking scenery, with its golden sand and clear waters framed by rocky headlands, creates a picture-perfect setting for family photos. Tuerredda also offers paddleboat rentals, allowing families to venture out onto the water and explore the coastline from a new perspective.

The island's family-friendly beaches are not just about safety and amenities—they also offer opportunities for exploration, adventure, and shared experiences. Many of these beaches are surrounded by natural parks, hiking trails, or historical sites, allowing families to combine a day at the beach with other activities. Whether it's spotting flamingos in a nearby lagoon, exploring ancient ruins, or simply enjoying a picnic under the shade of a Mediterranean pine, Sardinia's beaches provide a holistic experience that caters to every member of the family.

What makes Sardinia stand out as a family destination is its ability to balance natural beauty with practicality. The island's clean, well-maintained beaches and welcoming atmosphere ensure that families can relax and enjoy their time together without worry. Parents can feel confident in the safety of the beaches, while children are free to explore and play in an environment that encourages curiosity and discovery. Sardinia's family-friendly beaches are more than just places to swim—they are spaces where connections are deepened, memories are made, and the simple joys of life are celebrated.

Beach Safety and Etiquette

Beach safety and etiquette are essential aspects of enjoying the pristine shores of Sardinia while ensuring respect for the environment, local regulations, and other visitors. Whether you're a seasoned traveler or exploring the Mediterranean's beaches for the first time, understanding how to stay safe and act responsibly along this beautiful coastline is crucial. Sardinia's beaches, with their crystal-clear waters, soft sands, and dramatic landscapes, are natural treasures that deserve to be appreciated and preserved. By being mindful of safety guidelines and practicing proper etiquette, you can make your time on the beach enjoyable, stress-free, and considerate to others.

Safety begins with understanding the specific conditions and potential hazards of Sardinia's beaches. While many of the island's beaches are known for their calm, shallow waters, others can present challenges such as strong currents, sudden drops, or rocky outcrops. One of the most important things to look for upon arriving at a beach is the presence of a flag system, which is used to communicate water safety. A green flag indicates safe swimming conditions, while a yellow flag warns of caution due to moderate waves or currents. A red flag means swimming is prohibited, often due to dangerous rip currents or rough seas. Knowing this color-coded system and respecting it is vital, as even experienced swimmers can encounter difficulties in unfamiliar waters.

Another key aspect of beach safety is sun protection. Sardinia's Mediterranean climate means that the sun can be intense, particularly during the summer months. Without proper precautions, prolonged exposure can lead to painful sunburns, dehydration, or even heatstroke. Always bring and apply sunscreen with a high SPF, and reapply it regularly, especially after swimming. Wearing a wide-brimmed hat and UV-protective sunglasses can also help protect sensitive areas such as your face and eyes. For young children, rash guards or lightweight UV-blocking clothing are excellent options for additional coverage. Staying hydrated is equally important, so carry plenty of water to drink throughout the day, even if you don't feel particularly thirsty.

The calm appearance of Sardinia's waters can sometimes mask hidden dangers like underwater currents or sharp rocks. Certain beaches, particularly those in less-developed or remote areas, may lack lifeguards or clear signage, so it's important to assess the conditions yourself. If you're visiting a beach known for snorkeling or diving, wearing water shoes can help protect your feet from sharp rocks or sea urchins, which are common in some areas. If you're unsure about the safety of a particular spot, observe the locals or ask them for advice—they often have the best knowledge of the area's conditions.

When traveling with children, extra precautions are necessary to ensure their safety and enjoyment. Always keep a close eye on them, especially when they're near the water. Beaches with shallow, calm waters, such as La Cinta or Porto Giunco, are ideal for families, as they offer safe environments for kids to splash and play. Pack essentials like floatation devices or arm bands for younger children who are still learning to swim. Additionally, consider setting up your base close to lifeguard stations if available, as they provide an added layer of security.

Sardinia's marine environment is home to a wide variety of wildlife, including jellyfish, which can occasionally drift into swimming areas. While jellyfish stings are typically not life-threatening, they can be painful and uncomfortable. If you spot jellyfish in the water, it's best to avoid swimming in that area until the currents carry them away. In the event of a sting, rinse the affected area with seawater (not freshwater, as it can worsen the sting) and apply a soothing gel or cream to reduce irritation. Many beachside pharmacies stock products specifically designed for jellyfish stings, so it's worth having some on hand if you're visiting during peak jellyfish season.

Aside from personal safety, respecting the natural environment is a crucial part of beach etiquette. Sardinia's beaches are celebrated for their pristine beauty, and it's everyone's responsibility to ensure they remain that way for future generations. Always clean up after yourself, making sure to dispose of trash in designated bins or take it with you if no bins are available. This includes small items like cigarette butts or bottle caps, which can be harmful to marine life if left behind. If you see litter left by others, consider picking it up—a small act that contributes to the preservation of the beach's ecosystem.

Avoid disturbing the local flora and fauna, particularly in protected areas such as the La Maddalena Archipelago or beaches within natural parks. Many of these areas have regulations prohibiting the removal of sand, shells, or rocks, as they play a vital role in maintaining the ecological balance. For example, the famous pink sand of Budelli's Spiaggia Rosa has been protected for decades due to the damage caused by visitors taking sand as souvenirs. Respecting these rules not only helps preserve the environment but also demonstrates consideration for the local communities that depend on tourism.

Noise pollution is another aspect of beach etiquette that deserves attention. Sardinia's beaches are often cherished for their tranquility, and excessive noise can disrupt the peaceful atmosphere that many visitors come to enjoy. Whether you're playing music, chatting with friends, or setting up a children's game, be mindful of the volume so as not to disturb those around you. If you're planning a beach picnic, keep waste like paper plates or wrappers secure to prevent them from being blown away by the wind. A little mindfulness goes a long way in ensuring everyone can enjoy their time by the sea.

Dogs are welcome at certain beaches in Sardinia, but it's important to check in advance whether pets are allowed at the beach you plan to visit. For beaches that are dog-friendly, always keep your pet under control and clean up after them to maintain a pleasant environment for everyone. Many dog-friendly beaches also have specific rules, such as requiring dogs to remain on a leash or designating separate areas for pets and other beachgoers. Following these guidelines ensures a harmonious experience for all visitors.

If you're visiting one of Sardinia's more remote or hidden beaches, such as Cala Goloritzé or Cala Luna, remember that these locations often lack services like restrooms, restaurants, or lifeguards. Plan ahead by packing all the essentials you'll need for the day, including food, water, and a first-aid kit. Additionally, be prepared for physical effort, as many of these beaches require either a boat ride or a hike to access. The reward is well worth it, but respect the difficulty of the journey and ensure you're properly equipped.

For those exploring Sardinia by boat, anchoring etiquette is equally important. Many popular beaches have designated zones for anchoring to protect fragile marine habitats like seagrass meadows, which are vital for the ecosystem. Always follow local regulations and avoid anchoring in prohibited areas. If you're unsure, look for marked buoys or consult with local authorities to confirm the appropriate anchoring spots. Being mindful of these practices not only protects the environment but also ensures a safe and enjoyable boating experience.

Respecting local customs and cultural norms is an often-overlooked aspect of beach etiquette. While Sardinia is a welcoming destination, it's important to remember that some rural or less-touristy areas might have different expectations regarding behavior or dress. For instance, while swimwear is standard on the beach, it's considered inappropriate to wear swimsuits in restaurants or shops. Bringing a cover-up or change of clothes is a simple way to show respect for local sensibilities.

Beach safety and etiquette are not only about minimizing risks or following rules—they're about fostering a sense of responsibility and respect for the environment and the people around you. By being mindful of your actions and taking simple precautions, you can enjoy Sardinia's beaches to the fullest while helping preserve their beauty and charm. Whether you're exploring a hidden cove, relaxing on a family-friendly shoreline, or diving into the island's crystal-clear waters, practicing good safety habits and etiquette ensures that your time on Sardinia's coast is as rewarding as it is unforgettable.

CHAPTER 4: SARDINIA'S ANCIENT HISTORY AND ARCHAEOLOGICAL WONDERS

The Nuragic Civilization: Exploring the Nuraghe Towers

The Nuragic civilization, which flourished on Sardinia between approximately 1800 BCE and 500 BCE, left an enduring mark on the island's landscape, culture, and identity. At the heart of this enigmatic Bronze Age society were the nuraghe towers, monumental stone structures that stand as silent witnesses to a civilization that remains shrouded in mystery. These towers, numbering over 7,000 across the island, are not only architectural marvels but also crucial keys to understanding the lives, beliefs, and ingenuity of the Nuragic people. Exploring these ancient sites is like stepping into a time machine, offering glimpses into a world where human determination and creativity overcame the challenges of isolation and limited resources.

Nuraghi (plural of nuraghe) are unique to Sardinia, and their design has no direct parallel elsewhere in the ancient world. Built primarily from basalt, granite, or limestone, these towers were constructed using a technique known as cyclopean masonry, where large, irregular stones were carefully fitted together without the use of mortar. The result was a structure that was both durable and imposing, capable of withstanding centuries of weathering and seismic activity. Most nuraghi take the form of truncated cones, rising to heights of up to 20 meters, though their sizes and designs vary widely based on their purpose and the resources available in the surrounding area.

The function of nuraghi has been a subject of debate among archaeologists for decades. Some suggest they were defensive structures, designed to serve as fortresses or watchtowers that allowed the Nuragic people to monitor their territory and protect themselves from invaders. Others argue that nuraghi had a more communal or ceremonial role, serving as centers for religious rites or gatherings. Evidence suggests that many nuraghi were part of larger complexes that included villages, wells, and sacred spaces, indicating that they were integral to the social and spiritual life of the community. The duality of their potential purpose—both practical and symbolic—adds to their intrigue.

One of the most impressive nuraghi is Su Nuraxi in Barumini, located in the south-central part of the island. Designated a UNESCO World Heritage Site, Su Nuraxi is an extraordinary example of Nuragic engineering and social organization. The central tower, originally built around 1500 BCE, is surrounded by a complex of additional towers and walls that were added over the centuries, creating a labyrinthine structure that speaks to the evolution of the site. Excavations at Su Nuraxi have uncovered a wealth of artifacts, including pottery, tools, and weapons, providing valuable insights into the daily lives and trade networks of the Nuragic people. Walking through the site, it's impossible not to marvel at the ingenuity required to construct such a sophisticated complex with only rudimentary tools and technology.

Another remarkable site is Nuraghe Losa, located near the town of Abbasanta. This well-preserved nuraghe is notable for its massive, finely crafted stones and the precision with which they were assembled. The central tower is surrounded by a triangular courtyard and additional structures, creating a sense of both order and grandeur. Visitors to Nuraghe Losa can climb inside the tower and explore its interior chambers, which are connected by a spiral staircase carved into the stone. The experience of standing inside a space that was built thousands of years ago, yet still feels solid and enduring, is nothing short of awe-inspiring.

The nuraghi were not isolated monuments but part of a broader cultural landscape that included village settlements, sacred wells, and tombs. Sacred wells, such as the well of Santa Cristina near Paulilatino, are particularly fascinating. These wells, constructed with the same cyclopean masonry as the nuraghi, were meticulously engineered to provide access to water and may have held significant religious or symbolic meaning. Many sacred wells are aligned with celestial events, such as the solstices, suggesting that the Nuragic people had a sophisticated understanding of astronomy. The connection between water, fertility, and the divine was likely central to their worldview, making these wells important community landmarks.

Tombs of the giants, another hallmark of Nuragic culture, further illustrate the spiritual and communal priorities of this ancient civilization. These megalithic graves, named for their massive size rather than any association with actual giants, were communal burial sites that could hold the remains of dozens of individuals. Their construction, often involving large upright stones arranged in a semicircle or corridor, reflects the same architectural skill seen in the nuraghi. The tombs were likely places of ritual and remembrance, where the living could honor their ancestors and seek their guidance or protection.

The Nuragic civilization's interaction with other cultures is evident in the artifacts discovered at nuraghe sites. Bronze figurines, often depicting warriors, animals, or deities, are among the most iconic relics of this era. These figurines were likely used in religious ceremonies or as offerings, and their intricate craftsmanship suggests a high level of skill and artistic expression. Other artifacts, such as Mycenaean pottery or Phoenician beads, indicate that the Nuragic people were not isolated but engaged in trade and cultural exchange with other Mediterranean societies. This connection to the wider world adds another layer of complexity to the Nuragic story.

Visiting the nuraghi today is not just an exploration of ancient architecture but also an opportunity to connect with Sardinia's unique landscape. Many nuraghi are located in areas of stunning natural beauty, from rolling hills and fertile plains to rugged mountains and coastal cliffs. The relationship between the Nuragic people and their environment was one of interdependence, as they relied on the land for sustenance while shaping it to meet their needs. This harmony between human ingenuity and natural resources is still evident in Sardinia's rural landscapes, where traces of the past coexist with the rhythms of modern life.

The enduring presence of the nuraghi has also influenced Sardinian identity and folklore. These ancient structures are not just archaeological sites but symbols of resilience and continuity, representing a link between the island's distant past and its present. Stories and legends surrounding the nuraghi often speak of giants or other mythical beings who built these towers in a single night, imbuing the landscape with a sense of wonder and mystery. For many Sardinians, the nuraghi are a source of pride, a reminder of the island's rich heritage and the ingenuity of their ancestors.

Exploring the nuraghe towers is a journey into the heart of Sardinia's history, offering a deeper understanding of the island's cultural and architectural legacy. These structures, with their imposing presence and intricate designs, are a testament to human creativity and determination. They remind us that even in an age without modern technology, people could achieve remarkable feats, leaving behind a legacy that continues to inspire and captivate. For those who visit Sardinia, the nuraghi are more than just ancient ruins—they are a bridge to a civilization whose spirit endures in the stones they left behind.

The Giants of Mont'e Prama: Sardinia's Mysterious Statues

The Giants of Mont'e Prama are among Sardinia's most fascinating archaeological discoveries, shrouded in mystery and steeped in history. These monumental statues, carved from limestone, date back to the Iron Age and are believed to have been created by the Nuragic civilization, which dominated Sardinia for centuries. Found near the village of Cabras in the Sinis Peninsula, these statues have captured the imagination of historians, archaeologists, and visitors alike. Their imposing size, enigmatic features, and the questions surrounding their purpose make them an essential piece of Sardinia's cultural puzzle and a striking testament to the artistic and spiritual achievements of the island's ancient inhabitants.

The discovery of the Giants was almost accidental. In 1974, local farmers plowing their fields stumbled upon fragments of large stone sculptures buried beneath the soil. What initially looked like random pieces of carved rock soon revealed themselves to be parts of statues, each larger than life and intricately detailed. Excavations that followed uncovered more than 5,000 fragments, which archaeologists painstakingly pieced together over decades. The result was the reconstruction of around 30 statues, along with additional fragments that remain unassembled. These figures, now collectively known as the Giants of Mont'e Prama, represent one of the most significant archaeological finds in the Mediterranean and a unique cultural treasure for Sardinia.

The statues depict warriors, archers, boxers, and perhaps chieftains, each standing over two meters tall and exuding an air of power and authority. Their stylized features are striking: broad shoulders, elongated torsos, and large, circular eyes that seem to gaze into eternity. These eyes, carved as concentric circles, are one of the most distinctive elements of the Giants and have sparked much speculation about their meaning. Some scholars believe they symbolize divine vision or spiritual enlightenment, while others suggest they were simply an artistic convention unique to the Nuragic culture. Regardless of their interpretation, the eyes draw viewers in, creating an almost hypnotic connection between the statues and those who stand before them.

The craftsmanship of the Giants is remarkable, particularly given the tools and techniques available during the Iron Age. Carved from blocks of local limestone, the statues were sculpted with precision and attention to detail, from the folds of their clothing to the patterns of their armor. The boxers, for example, are depicted with shields raised above their heads, a stance that conveys both readiness and defiance. The warriors hold swords and wear helmets adorned with horns, emphasizing their martial prowess. The archers, meanwhile, are shown with bows slung over their shoulders and quivers at their sides, their postures suggesting vigilance and control. Each statue is unique, yet they all share a sense of purpose and unity, as if they were part of a larger narrative or ritual.

The purpose of the Giants remains one of the greatest mysteries surrounding them. Some theories suggest that they were guardians of a sacred site, perhaps standing watch over a temple or necropolis. This idea is supported by the discovery of tombs near the site where the statues were found, indicating that Mont'e Prama may have been a significant burial ground for the Nuragic elite. The statues could have served as a way to honor the dead, representing ancestral spirits or deities tasked with protecting the living and the departed. Alternatively, they may have been symbols of power and prestige, erected to demonstrate the strength and sophistication of the Nuragic civilization to both insiders and outsiders.

Another intriguing possibility is that the Giants were part of a larger religious or ceremonial complex. The Sinis Peninsula, with its proximity to the sea and fertile lands, was an important area for the Nuragic people, and Mont'e Prama may have been a center of spiritual activity. The statues' imposing size and dramatic appearance would have made them ideal focal points for rituals or gatherings, inspiring awe and reverence among those who saw them. Their placement along a route or axis could have guided pilgrims or marked a boundary between the mundane and the sacred.

The discovery of the Giants has also raised questions about the influence and connections of the Nuragic civilization within the broader Mediterranean world. Some scholars see parallels between the Mont'e Prama statues and the kouroi of ancient Greece, the freestanding statues of male youths that appeared during the Archaic period. While the stylistic similarities are intriguing, there is little evidence to suggest direct contact between the Nuragic people and the Greeks. Instead, the resemblance may reflect shared artistic traditions or independent developments influenced by similar cultural and environmental factors. What is clear, however, is that the Giants represent a distinct and original artistic achievement, rooted in the unique context of Sardinian history and society.

The significance of the Giants extends beyond their artistic and historical value. They also offer insights into the social structure and values of the Nuragic civilization. The emphasis on warriors and archers suggests a society that placed a high value on strength, skill, and the ability to protect and defend. At the same time, the presence of boxers indicates an appreciation for athleticism and perhaps a tradition of ritual combat or sport. The statues' size and craftsmanship suggest that they were commissioned by a wealthy and powerful elite, capable of mobilizing the resources and labor needed to create such monumental works. This speaks to a level of organization and hierarchy within Nuragic society that is still not fully understood.

Today, the Giants of Mont'e Prama are housed in the Giovanni Marongiu Museum in Cabras, where visitors can view the reconstructed statues alongside other artifacts from the site. The museum provides context and interpretation, helping to bring the story of the Giants to life. Seeing the statues up close is a powerful experience, allowing viewers to appreciate their scale, detail, and the skill of the artisans who created them. The museum also highlights the ongoing efforts to study and preserve the Giants, as new discoveries and technologies continue to shed light on their origins and significance.

The Giants have also become a symbol of Sardinian identity and pride, representing the island's rich cultural heritage and its connection to the past. For many Sardinians, the statues are more than just archaeological artifacts—they are a link to their ancestors and a reminder of the creativity and resilience that have defined their history. The Giants have inspired artists, writers, and musicians, becoming a source of inspiration and a point of connection between generations.

The story of the Giants of Mont'e Prama is far from complete. As archaeologists continue to study the site and its artifacts, new questions and possibilities emerge, adding layers of complexity to our understanding of these enigmatic statues. What is certain is that the Giants stand as a testament to the skill, imagination, and spirit of the Nuragic civilization. They remind us of the power of art to transcend time, connecting us to a world that existed thousands of years ago yet still resonates today. For those who visit Sardinia, the Giants offer an opportunity to engage with a profound and mysterious legacy, one that continues to inspire wonder and discovery.

Roman and Phoenician Ruins

Sardinia's history is a tapestry woven from the influence of many civilizations, and among the most significant are the Romans and the Phoenicians. Their presence on the island has left an indelible mark, particularly through the ruins that remain scattered across the landscape. These remnants of ancient cities, ports, and temples offer glimpses into a time when Sardinia was not just an isolated island but a vital hub in the Mediterranean world. Exploring these ruins is akin to walking through the pages of history, where every stone and column tells a story of trade, conquest, cultural exchange, and adaptation to the island's unique environment.

The Phoenicians were among the first major external powers to establish a significant presence in Sardinia, arriving on the island around the 9th century BCE. Renowned as master sailors and traders, the Phoenicians were drawn to Sardinia's strategic location in the western Mediterranean, which made it an ideal stopover on their trade routes. They founded settlements primarily along the coast, choosing locations that offered safe harbors and access to natural resources. One of the most notable of these settlements is Tharros, located on the Sinis Peninsula near the modern town of Cabras. Tharros became a thriving center of commerce, its position between the sea and the fertile hinterlands offering abundant opportunities for trade and agriculture.

Walking through the ruins of Tharros today, it's easy to imagine the bustle of a Phoenician port city. The site is perched on a scenic promontory overlooking the Gulf of Oristano, with sweeping views of the coastline and the surrounding landscape. Among the most striking features of Tharros are its remnants of ancient streets, lined with the foundations of shops and houses that once bustled with activity. The Phoenicians, known for their pragmatic urban planning, laid out the city with a clear sense of organization, using stone-paved streets and drainage systems that highlight their advanced engineering skills. Excavations at the site have uncovered an array of artifacts, from pottery and tools to jewelry and inscriptions, offering insights into the daily lives of its inhabitants.

Central to Tharros is its sacred area, where the remains of a tophet, a type of open-air sanctuary typical of Phoenician culture, have been discovered. The tophet was used for religious rituals, including offerings to deities such as Tanit and Baal Hammon, who were central figures in the Phoenician pantheon. Stone stelae and urns found at the site bear witness to these ceremonies, which may have included the sacrifice of animals or other offerings. The spiritual significance of Tharros persisted even after the Phoenicians were succeeded by other powers, as the city's temples and sanctuaries continued to be used and adapted by later civilizations.

The arrival of the Romans in Sardinia in 238 BCE marked the beginning of a new chapter in the island's history. Following the First Punic War, Sardinia became a Roman province, and the Romans wasted no time in asserting their control and integrating the island into their vast empire. They expanded existing cities, introduced new infrastructure, and exploited Sardinia's resources, particularly its grain and minerals, which were vital to Rome's economy. The Roman influence can still be seen in the island's architecture, engineering, and urban planning, much of which was designed to facilitate the efficient administration and exploitation of the province.

One of the most impressive examples of Roman ruins in Sardinia is the ancient city of Nora, located near Pula on the island's southern coast. Nora is believed to be one of the oldest cities in Sardinia, originally founded by the Phoenicians and later expanded by the Romans. The site's location on a triangular promontory jutting into the sea made it a natural choice for a port and settlement. Today, Nora is a sprawling archaeological site that offers a fascinating glimpse into Roman urban life. Visitors can explore the remains of a theater, thermal baths, temples, and private residences, all of which showcase the characteristic features of Roman architecture.

The theater at Nora is particularly well-preserved and remains a focal point of the site. Built to accommodate hundreds of spectators, it reflects the importance of public entertainment and cultural life in Roman cities. The semicircular seating area, orchestra, and stage are still visible, and the theater continues to host performances and events, connecting the past with the present. Nearby, the thermal baths reveal the sophistication of Roman engineering, with their intricate heating systems and mosaic floors. These baths were not just places for hygiene but also social hubs where citizens gathered to relax, converse, and conduct business.

The mosaics at Nora are among its most captivating features, showcasing the artistry and craftsmanship of the Roman period. These intricate designs, often depicting scenes of mythology, nature, or geometric patterns, adorned the floors of wealthy residences and public buildings. The mosaics provide a window into the aesthetics and values of Roman society, reflecting a culture that valued beauty, order, and symbolism. Walking among these ruins, it's impossible not to feel a sense of connection to the people who once lived, worked, and celebrated in this ancient city.

Another remarkable Roman site is the amphitheater of Cagliari, the island's capital. Carved into a limestone hillside, the amphitheater could accommodate thousands of spectators and was used for gladiatorial games, animal hunts, and public spectacles. Its elliptical shape and tiered seating are characteristic of Roman amphitheaters, designed to provide optimal views for the audience. Although time and quarrying activities have taken their toll on the structure, it remains an iconic landmark and a testament to Roman engineering and entertainment culture. Nearby, the Roman Villa of Tigellio offers further insights into the domestic life of the era, with its courtyards, frescoes, and mosaics hinting at the opulence enjoyed by Sardinia's elite.

The Roman road network in Sardinia, though less visible today, was another crucial aspect of their legacy. These roads connected cities, ports, and rural areas, facilitating trade, communication, and military movement. Traces of these ancient routes can still be found in the landscape, often forming the basis for modern roads. The Roman emphasis on infrastructure not only enhanced the island's economic potential but also left a lasting imprint on its geography and development.

While the ruins of Sardinia's Phoenician and Roman past are undeniably captivating, they also raise important questions about the interactions between these cultures and the island's indigenous Nuragic people. The extent to which the Nuragic civilization adapted to or resisted these external influences remains a topic of debate among scholars. Artifacts and architectural elements suggest a degree of cultural exchange, yet the Nuragic identity persisted long after the arrival of the Phoenicians and Romans. This interplay of continuity and change adds depth to the story of Sardinia's ancient history, highlighting the complexity of its cultural heritage.

Visiting these ruins is not just an opportunity to admire ancient architecture but also a chance to reflect on the resilience and adaptability of the people who lived on Sardinia throughout its tumultuous history. The Phoenicians and Romans, though separated by centuries, both recognized the island's strategic importance and left their mark in ways that continue to shape its identity. Their ruins stand as reminders of Sardinia's place in the broader narrative of Mediterranean civilization, a crossroads where cultures met, clashed, and merged.

The legacy of these ancient civilizations extends beyond the stones and artifacts they left behind. They are woven into the consciousness of Sardinia's people, who take pride in the island's rich and diverse history. The ruins of Tharros, Nora, and Cagliari are not just tourist attractions; they are symbols of a heritage that has endured through millennia, a testament to the ingenuity and vision of those who came before. For visitors, exploring these sites is a journey through time, an invitation to connect with the stories and achievements of the past while appreciating the beauty and complexity of Sardinia's cultural landscape.

Sacred Wells and Ancient Temples

Sardinia's landscape is not only defined by its rugged mountains, pristine beaches, and rolling plains but also by the remarkable sacred wells and ancient temples scattered across the island. These structures, remnants of the Nuragic civilization, reveal a deep connection between the people of ancient Sardinia and their spiritual beliefs, as well as their ability to harmonize architecture with the natural world. Sacred wells and temples served as focal points for rituals, gatherings, and expressions of devotion, often tied to water,

125

fertility, and celestial events. Exploring these sites offers a profound understanding of the spiritual life of the Nuragic people, as well as their architectural ingenuity and the cultural significance they placed on their environment.

Sacred wells, known as "pozzi sacri," are among the most intriguing and enigmatic relics of the Nuragic civilization. These wells were not merely functional sources of water but held significant religious and symbolic value. Constructed with cyclopean masonry, the same dry-stone technique used for nuraghi, these wells were carefully engineered to access groundwater while maintaining a precise and aesthetically pleasing design. One of the most remarkable features of sacred wells is their alignment with astronomical events, suggesting that the Nuragic people possessed advanced knowledge of the heavens. These wells often served as places of worship, where rituals were performed to honor deities associated with water, fertility, and the cycles of nature.

The well of Santa Cristina, located near the village of Paulilatino, is one of Sardinia's most iconic sacred wells. This site is a masterpiece of Nuragic engineering and spirituality, consisting of a subterranean chamber accessed by a perfectly symmetrical staircase made of basalt. The staircase leads to a trapezoidal vestibule and then to the circular well chamber, where water reflects the light that filters through the carefully constructed opening above. The precision of the construction is astonishing, with the stones fitting together seamlessly despite the absence of mortar. The well's alignment with the moon is another striking feature; during certain phases of the lunar cycle, the moonlight shines directly into the well, illuminating the water below. This alignment has led scholars to believe that the well was used for lunar-related rituals or as an observatory to mark significant celestial events.

The sacred well of Santa Cristina is part of a larger complex that includes a Nuragic village and a rectangular temple. The temple, with its elongated shape and central hearth, may have been used for rituals involving fire or offerings. This combination of water and fire in the same sacred area reflects the duality and balance often found in ancient spiritual practices, where opposing elements were seen as interconnected forces of creation and renewal. The overall layout of the site suggests that it was a place of great importance, attracting pilgrims from across the island for ceremonies and communal gatherings.

Another extraordinary sacred well is Su Tempiesu, located near Orune. Unlike Santa Cristina, Su Tempiesu is partially carved into a rocky hillside, blending seamlessly with the surrounding landscape. The rectangular vestibule, built with precision-cut stones, leads to the well chamber, which is enclosed by a sloping roof that channels rainwater into the basin below. The design of Su Tempiesu demonstrates not only the Nuragic people's architectural skill but also their ability to integrate their structures into the natural environment. The site's remote location, surrounded by verdant hills and flowing streams, adds to its mystique, creating an atmosphere of serenity and reverence.

The significance of sacred wells extends beyond their architectural and astronomical features. These sites were deeply intertwined with the daily lives and beliefs of the Nuragic people, serving as places where they sought divine favor for fertility, agriculture, and protection. Offerings of pottery, bronze figurines, and other artifacts have been found at many well sites, indicating that they were used for votive practices. The presence of these objects suggests that worshippers sought to establish a connection with the divine, expressing gratitude or petitioning for blessings. The act of leaving an offering, often in the form of a carefully crafted object, underscores the importance of these wells as sacred spaces where the material and spiritual worlds intersected.

In addition to sacred wells, ancient temples played a central role in Nuragic spirituality. These temples, which often feature a megaron-like design with rectangular or trapezoidal layouts, were places of worship dedicated to various deities or natural forces. The temple of Malchittu, near Arzachena in northern Sardinia, is a prime example of this architectural style. Nestled in a tranquil valley, the temple consists of a rectangular chamber with a central altar and a semi-circular forecourt. The site's alignment with the surrounding hills and its proximity to a water source suggest that it was carefully chosen for its symbolic and practical significance. The temple's design emphasizes simplicity and functionality, reflecting a spiritual practice that was deeply connected to the rhythms of nature.

Another noteworthy site is the temple of Monte d'Accoddi, located near Sassari. Often described as Sardinia's "Ziggurat," Monte d'Accoddi is a unique and enigmatic structure that predates the Nuragic civilization but continued to be used and adapted by later cultures. The site features a stepped platform with a ramp leading to its summit, where rituals were likely performed. Surrounding the platform are various altars and ceremonial spaces, indicating that the site was a focal point for religious activity. The presence of animal bones and other sacrificial remains suggests that offerings played a central role in the rituals conducted here. Monte d'Accoddi's distinctive design and its parallels with Mesopotamian ziggurats have sparked debates about the cultural influences that shaped its construction, adding an extra layer of intrigue to this ancient temple.

The temples and sacred wells of Sardinia were not isolated structures but part of a broader spiritual landscape that included nuraghi, tombs of the giants, and other ceremonial sites. These interconnected elements reflect a holistic worldview in which the natural and supernatural were inseparable. The Nuragic people's reverence for water, stone, and the celestial sphere is evident in the care and precision with which they constructed their sacred spaces. This reverence extended to their rituals, which likely involved music, dance, and communal feasting, creating a sense of unity and shared purpose among participants.

The legacy of Sardinia's sacred wells and ancient temples continues to resonate today, providing a window into a world where spirituality and daily life were deeply intertwined. These sites are not just archaeological relics but enduring symbols of a culture that valued harmony with nature and the cosmos. For visitors, exploring these sacred spaces offers a chance to connect with the island's ancient heritage, to marvel at the ingenuity of its people, and to reflect on the universal human quest for meaning and transcendence.

The sacred wells and temples of Sardinia stand as a testament to the ingenuity, spirituality, and resilience of the Nuragic civilization. Their enduring presence in the landscape is a reminder of the deep connections between humanity, nature, and the divine, connections that continue to inspire and captivate those who walk among these ancient stones. For those who seek to understand Sardinia's past, these sites offer not only historical insights but also a profound sense of wonder and reverence for the mysteries of life and the universe.

Sardinia's Medieval Castles and Churches

Sardinia's medieval castles and churches stand as enduring symbols of a time when the island was shaped by the influence of powerful kingdoms, relentless invaders, and a deep-rooted devotion to faith. These structures, scattered across the landscape, tell the story of an island caught between conflicting forces yet steadfast in preserving its cultural identity. Built for defense, governance, or worship, these castles and churches are not merely relics of the past but living monuments that continue to define Sardinia's character. Exploring these sites offers a journey through the Middle Ages, revealing the artistry, ingenuity, and resilience of the people who constructed them.

The castles of Sardinia, often perched on rugged cliffs or hilltops, were primarily built during the period of the Giudicati, the four independent judicial kingdoms that ruled the island between the 9th and 15th centuries. These fortresses served as defensive strongholds, administrative centers, and symbols of power. Castles such as Castello di Sanluri, Castello di Acquafredda, and Castello di Serravalle (also known as Castello di Bosa) exemplify the strategic importance and architectural prowess of medieval Sardinia. Their enduring presence, even in ruins, speaks to the formidable challenges of the era and the determination of the rulers who sought to protect their domains.

Castello di Sanluri, located in the southern part of the island, is one of the best-preserved castles in Sardinia. Built in the 14th century by the Giudicato of Arborea, it played a crucial role in the island's political and military history. Its strategic position allowed it to control the surrounding plains and serve as a defensive bastion against external threats. Today, the castle houses a museum that offers visitors a glimpse into medieval life, with exhibits featuring weapons, armor, and artifacts from the period. Walking through its halls, one can imagine the tension and intrigue that once filled these walls as rulers and soldiers strategized to protect their lands.

In contrast, Castello di Acquafredda, situated near Siliqua, is a more enigmatic structure. Perched on a volcanic hill, the castle was built in the 13th century by the Pisan nobleman Ugolino della Gherardesca, whose tragic story is immortalized in Dante's "Divine Comedy." The ruins of Acquafredda offer breathtaking views of the surrounding landscape, a testament to its strategic location. Exploring the castle's remains, including its walls, towers, and cisterns, provides a sense of the challenges faced by those who lived and worked there, from withstanding sieges to enduring the harsh realities of medieval warfare.

Castello di Serravalle, overlooking the charming town of Bosa, is another remarkable example of Sardinia's medieval architecture. Built in the 12th century by the Malaspina family, this castle served as both a defensive stronghold and a residence for the ruling elite. Its position atop a hill provided a commanding view of the Temo River and the surrounding valley, ensuring control over the region's trade routes. The castle's chapel, Santa Maria de Sos Regnos Altos, is a highlight of the site, featuring well-preserved frescoes that depict religious scenes and offer insight into the spiritual life of the period. The combination of military and religious elements at Serravalle reflects the dual priorities of protection and piety that defined medieval Sardinia.

While the castles of Sardinia were built to defend and dominate, its medieval churches were constructed to inspire and unite. These sacred spaces, ranging from simple rural chapels to grand cathedrals, reflect the island's deep Christian heritage and the influence of various architectural styles, including Romanesque, Gothic, and Byzantine. Many of these churches were built during the period of the Giudicati, as rulers sought to assert their authority not only through military might but also through religious patronage. The churches of Sardinia stand as testaments to the skill of their builders and the faith of their communities.

The Basilica di San Gavino in Porto Torres is one of Sardinia's most significant medieval churches. Built in the 11th century, this Romanesque basilica is the largest and oldest of its kind on the island. Constructed from local limestone and granite, its simple yet imposing design reflects the Romanesque emphasis on solidity and grandeur. Inside, the basilica's three naves are supported by columns and arches that create a sense of harmony and balance. The crypt, which houses the relics of Saints Gavino, Proto, and Gianuario, adds to the church's spiritual significance, making it a place of pilgrimage and devotion.

Another remarkable example of medieval ecclesiastical architecture is the Cathedral of Santa Maria di Castello in Cagliari. Situated within the city's historic Castello district, this cathedral has undergone numerous renovations and expansions since its construction in the 13th century. As a result, it features a blend of architectural styles, including Romanesque, Gothic, and Baroque. The cathedral's interior is adorned with intricate marble work, frescoes, and sculptures, showcasing the artistic achievements of the period. The crypt, known as the Sanctuary of the Martyrs, contains the remains of early Christian martyrs and provides a poignant connection to Sardinia's religious history.

In the heart of the Giudicato of Arborea lies the Church of San Pietro di Sorres, a stunning example of Romanesque architecture. Perched on a hill near the town of Borutta, this church is notable for its black and white striped façade, created using alternating layers of basalt and limestone. The interior features a simple yet elegant design, with a single nave and a semicircular apse. Today, San Pietro di Sorres is home to a Benedictine monastery, where monks continue to uphold centuries-old traditions of prayer and hospitality. The church's serene setting and timeless beauty make it a place of reflection and spiritual renewal.

The Church of San Michele in Ozieri offers a different perspective on medieval Sardinian architecture. This small rural church, built in the 12th century, is a fine example of the Pisan-Romanesque style that was introduced to Sardinia by the maritime republic of Pisa. Its modest size and unadorned design contrast with the grandeur of larger cathedrals, yet its simplicity conveys a sense of intimacy and devotion. The church's location, surrounded by rolling hills and pastures, adds to its charm, creating a sense of connection between the sacred and the natural world.

The interplay between castles and churches in medieval Sardinia reflects the complex dynamics of power, faith, and community. While castles symbolized the authority and strength of the ruling elite, churches served as centers of spiritual life and social cohesion. Together, these structures reveal a society that was both deeply hierarchical and profoundly connected to its religious traditions. The coexistence of these elements in the Sardinian landscape speaks to the resilience and adaptability of its people, who navigated the challenges of the Middle Ages while preserving their cultural identity.

Today, Sardinia's medieval castles and churches continue to captivate visitors with their beauty, history, and significance. These sites are not just remnants of the past but living monuments that offer insights into the island's heritage and the values of its people. Exploring these structures is an opportunity to step back in time, to imagine the lives of those who built and inhabited them, and to appreciate the enduring legacy of Sardinia's medieval era. For anyone seeking to understand the soul of this remarkable island, its castles and churches provide a window into a world where faith and fortitude shaped the course of history.

CHAPTER 5: OUTDOOR ADVENTURES AND NATURAL ATTRACTIONS

Hiking in Sardinia: Trails for All Levels

Sardinia's rugged and varied landscape makes it a paradise for hikers, offering trails that cater to all levels of fitness and experience. Whether you're an avid trekker seeking a challenging multi-day route or a casual walker eager to enjoy a leisurely stroll through nature, Sardinia has something for you. From dramatic coastal cliffs and ancient forests to remote mountain ranges and hidden archaeological sites, the island's trails provide a unique opportunity to connect with its natural beauty and cultural heritage. Hiking in Sardinia is not just an outdoor activity; it's a journey into the heart of this extraordinary Mediterranean island, where every step reveals a new layer of its diverse geography and rich history.

For those new to hiking or simply looking for an easy, accessible walk, Sardinia offers trails that balance scenic beauty with manageable terrain. One such trail is the trek to Cala Luna, a stunning beach on the eastern coast of the island. Starting from the village of Cala Gonone, this trail winds through a landscape of limestone hills, fragrant Mediterranean scrub, and occasional glimpses of the turquoise sea. The path is well-marked and relatively flat, making it suitable for beginners and families. Along the way, hikers can enjoy the shade of ancient juniper trees and the sound of birdsong, creating a tranquil atmosphere that culminates in the breathtaking sight of Cala Luna's crescent-shaped bay. The pristine beach, with its golden sand and caves carved into the cliffs, is a reward well worth the effort.

Another excellent option for beginners is the Molentargius Trail near Cagliari. This route takes you through the Molentargius-Saline Regional Park, a protected wetland area known for its population of pink flamingos. The trail is flat and easy to navigate, making it perfect for those who want to combine a gentle walk with wildlife observation. As you stroll along the paths, you'll pass salt pans, lagoons, and reed beds, all teeming with birdlife. The park's proximity to the city means you can enjoy a peaceful escape into nature without venturing too far from urban amenities. It's a reminder of how Sardinia's natural wonders are often just a short distance from its towns and cities.

For intermediate hikers looking for more variety and challenge, the Selvaggio Blu is a must-experience trail. While the full route is one of the most demanding in Europe, there are sections that can be tackled by moderately experienced hikers as day trips. This legendary trail runs along the wild and remote coastline of the Supramonte in eastern Sardinia, offering a mix of rocky paths, steep descents, and breathtaking views of the Tyrrhenian Sea. The segment from Cala Fuili to Cala Biriola, for instance, combines manageable climbs with rewarding vistas and the chance to explore secluded beaches. Along the way, you'll encounter ancient shepherds' huts and dry-stone walls, remnants of Sardinia's pastoral history that add a cultural dimension to the hike.

Monte Arci, located in the central-western part of Sardinia, is another fantastic destination for intermediate hikers. This extinct volcanic massif is known for its deposits of obsidian, a volcanic glass that was highly valued in prehistoric times for making tools. The trails on Monte Arci are rich in both natural and archaeological interest, winding through forests of cork oak and Mediterranean maquis. One of the most popular routes leads to Sa Domu e S'Orcu, a megalithic tomb that dates back to the Nuragic era. The panoramic views from the summit, which stretch across the Campidano plain to the Gulf of Oristano, make the climb particularly rewarding.

Advanced hikers seeking a true test of endurance and skill will find no shortage of challenges in Sardinia's mountainous regions. The climb to Punta La Marmora, the highest peak on the island, is a rite of passage for serious trekkers. Located in the Gennargentu massif in central Sardinia, this trail offers a demanding ascent through rugged terrain, but the rewards are unparalleled. Standing at 1,834 meters above sea level, Punta La Marmora provides sweeping views that stretch from the coastline to the rolling hills and valleys of the interior. The trail also passes through diverse ecosystems, from alpine meadows dotted with wildflowers to rocky outcrops that are home to golden eagles and mouflons, Sardinia's native wild sheep.

Another challenging yet unforgettable hike is the trek to Gorropu Gorge, often referred to as the "Grand Canyon of Europe." This dramatic limestone canyon, located in the Supramonte, plunges to depths of over 500 meters and is flanked by sheer cliffs that seem to touch the sky. The trail begins near the Flumineddu River and gradually ascends through rocky paths and dense vegetation before reaching the entrance to the gorge. Once inside, hikers are dwarfed by the towering walls and can explore the labyrinth of boulders and caves that make up this natural wonder. The hike requires stamina and good footwear, but the sense of awe you'll feel standing at the bottom of Gorropu Gorge is worth every step.

Sardinia's hiking trails are not just about the physical journey; they are also a gateway to the island's cultural and historical treasures. Many routes pass by Nuragic ruins, ancient churches, and traditional villages, offering a glimpse into the lives of the people who have inhabited this land for millennia. The trail to Tiscali, a hidden Nuragic village located in a sinkhole in the Supramonte, is a perfect example. The hike to Tiscali combines steep climbs and narrow paths with the reward of discovering a site that feels frozen in time. The ruins, partially concealed by the limestone walls of the sinkhole, speak to the ingenuity and resilience of the Nuragic people, who sought refuge in this secluded spot.

As you hike through Sardinia, you'll also encounter its unique flora and fauna, which add another layer of richness to the experience. The island is home to a variety of plant species, from aromatic herbs like rosemary and thyme to rare orchids that bloom in the spring. Wildlife enthusiasts may spot Sardinian deer, wild boar, or even the elusive monk seal along the coast. Birdwatchers will be delighted by the sight of peregrine falcons, griffon vultures, and the vibrant bee-eaters that frequent the island's skies. The diversity of Sardinia's ecosystems ensures that every trail offers something new to discover.

Preparing for a hike in Sardinia requires careful planning to ensure a safe and enjoyable experience. The island's climate can vary significantly depending on the season and altitude, so it's important to dress appropriately and carry essentials such as water, sunscreen, and a map or GPS device. Many trails pass through remote areas with limited access to facilities, so packing snacks and a basic first aid kit is also advisable. While some routes are well-marked, others require a guide or detailed knowledge of the terrain, especially in regions like the Supramonte where paths can be difficult to follow.

Hiking in Sardinia is more than a recreational activity; it's an opportunity to immerse yourself in the island's natural beauty, connect with its history, and experience the tranquility of its remote landscapes. Whether you're walking along a coastal path, climbing a mountain peak, or exploring an ancient ruin, each trail offers a unique perspective on Sardinia's diverse geography and cultural heritage. The island's trails cater to all levels, ensuring that everyone, from casual walkers to seasoned trekkers, can find a route that speaks to their sense of adventure. Sardinia invites you to lace up your boots, step onto its trails, and discover a world where nature and history converge in breathtaking harmony.

Gennargentu National Park: Sardinia's Wild Heart

Gennargentu National Park, a sprawling expanse of rugged peaks, verdant valleys, and untamed wilderness, represents the wild heart of Sardinia. Covering a vast area in the island's central-eastern region, it is home to Sardinia's highest mountains, including Punta La Marmora and Bruncu Spina, as well as deep gorges, pristine rivers, and rare flora and fauna. This protected area is not only a haven for nature lovers and outdoor enthusiasts but also a critical repository of the island's ecological and cultural heritage. Visiting Gennargentu National Park is an invitation to step into an ancient landscape, untouched by time, where the rhythms of nature still dominate and every corner tells a story of resilience, beauty, and life in its rawest form.

The park's name, Gennargentu, translates loosely to "Silver Gate," a poetic reference to the silvery hues of its peaks as they catch the sunlight at dawn and dusk. These mountains, formed millions of years ago, rise dramatically from the surrounding plains, their craggy slopes carved by millennia of wind and water. Punta La Marmora, standing at 1,834 meters, is the highest point on the island and offers breathtaking views that stretch across Sardinia and, on clear days, even to the distant Tyrrhenian Sea. The climb to the summit is challenging but immensely rewarding, taking hikers through a landscape that shifts from dense forests to open alpine meadows, each step revealing a new facet of the park's diverse ecosystem.

The Gennargentu range is not just about lofty peaks; it is also home to landscapes of extraordinary variety and contrast. The Supramonte region, which borders the park to the east, is a labyrinth of limestone plateaus, steep cliffs, and hidden caves. Among its most famous features is Gorropu Gorge, one of the deepest canyons in Europe. Dropping to depths of over 500 meters, the gorge is a marvel of geology and a sanctuary for rare species such as the golden eagle and the Sardinian wildcat. Exploring Gorropu requires a mix of stamina and curiosity, as the journey into its depths takes you through a world of towering rock walls and boulder-strewn pathways, where silence is broken only by the occasional rustle of wildlife or the whisper of the wind.

The rivers and streams that flow through Gennargentu National Park are lifelines for its ecosystems, nourishing both the land and its inhabitants. The Flumendosa River, one of

Sardinia's longest waterways, originates in the park and winds its way through valleys and gorges before emptying into the sea. Its crystal-clear waters are home to diverse aquatic life, including trout and freshwater crabs, and provide essential hydration for the park's wildlife. Smaller streams, often fed by natural springs, form picturesque waterfalls and pools that invite moments of reflection and respite for visitors. These waterways also play a vital role in sustaining the lush vegetation that blankets much of the park, from cork oak forests to carpets of wildflowers.

The flora of Gennargentu is as varied as its terrain, with plant species that range from hardy shrubs to delicate blooms. The lower slopes of the mountains are covered in Mediterranean maquis, a dense mix of aromatic plants such as myrtle, rosemary, and juniper. As you ascend, the vegetation changes, giving way to oak and holm oak forests that provide shade and shelter for countless creatures. Higher still, the landscape becomes more open, with alpine meadows dotted with rare flowers such as the Sardinian violet and the snowbell. These plants, many of which are endemic to the island, have adapted to the harsh conditions of the mountains, their beauty a testament to nature's resilience.

The wildlife of Gennargentu National Park is equally remarkable, offering a glimpse into a world where nature still reigns supreme. Large mammals such as the Sardinian deer and mouflon roam the park's forests and meadows, their movements graceful yet elusive. The golden eagle, with its majestic wingspan, soars above the peaks, a symbol of the park's untamed spirit. Smaller creatures, from foxes to dormice, thrive in the undergrowth, while a chorus of birdsong adds a melodic backdrop to the natural symphony.

Amphibians such as the Sardinian newt and reptiles like the Hermann's tortoise also make their home here, their presence a reminder of the park's ecological richness and importance.

Gennargentu National Park is not just a refuge for wildlife; it is also a living museum of Sardinia's ancient history and traditions. Scattered throughout the park are Nuragic ruins, the remnants of a civilization that flourished on the island thousands of years ago. These structures, ranging from stone towers to burial sites, offer a window into the lives and beliefs of Sardinia's early inhabitants. The park is also dotted with shepherds' huts, known as pinnettos, which have been used for centuries as shelters by those who tend flocks in the mountains. These simple yet ingenious structures, made of stone and wood, are a testament to the enduring connection between the island's people and its rugged landscape.

The human history of Gennargentu is deeply intertwined with its natural environment, and this relationship continues to shape the lives of those who call the region home. Traditional practices such as sheep herding and the production of pecorino cheese remain an integral part of the local economy and culture. Visitors to the park can often encounter shepherds tending their flocks or taste the fruits of their labor in the form of artisanal cheeses and other delicacies. These interactions provide a unique opportunity to learn about Sardinia's heritage and the ways in which its people have adapted to and thrived in this challenging environment.

For those seeking adventure, Gennargentu National Park offers a wealth of activities that allow you to immerse yourself in its wild beauty. Hiking is perhaps the most popular way to explore the park, with trails that range from easy walks to strenuous climbs. The trek to Punta La Marmora is a favorite among experienced hikers, while the paths around Monte Spada and Bruncu Spina offer more accessible options with equally stunning views. Mountain biking and horseback riding are also excellent ways to navigate the park's diverse terrain, providing a sense of freedom and connection to the land.

The park's rivers and streams invite opportunities for kayaking, fishing, and even wild swimming, while its cliffs and caves attract climbers and spelunkers eager to test their skills. For those who prefer a more leisurely pace, guided tours and nature walks provide insights into the park's flora, fauna, and geology, often led by knowledgeable locals who share their passion for the region. Whether you're scaling a peak, tracing the course of a river, or simply soaking in the serenity of a meadow, the experiences offered by Gennargentu National Park are as varied as its landscapes.

Visiting Gennargentu requires preparation and respect for the environment. The park's remote location and rugged terrain mean that facilities are limited, so it's essential to carry sufficient water, food, and appropriate gear for your chosen activity. Weather conditions can change rapidly in the mountains, so dressing in layers and being prepared for sudden shifts in temperature are crucial. Many trails are unmarked or poorly signposted, making a map or GPS device indispensable, especially for those venturing off the beaten path. Above all, visitors are encouraged to tread lightly, leaving no trace of their presence to ensure that this pristine wilderness remains unspoiled for future generations.

Gennargentu National Park is more than a destination; it is an experience that stays with you long after you leave. Its rugged beauty, ecological diversity, and cultural significance create a sense of awe and wonder that is difficult to put into words.

Here, amid the silence of the peaks and the whispers of the forests, you can feel the pulse of Sardinia's wild heart, a rhythm that connects the past to the present and the natural world to the human spirit. For those who seek adventure, discovery, or simply a moment of peace, Gennargentu offers a glimpse into a world where nature reigns supreme and life unfolds in its purest form.

Exploring Sardinian Caves: Grotta di Nettuno and Beyond

Beneath the rugged surface of Sardinia lies a hidden world of extraordinary beauty, mystery, and geological wonder. The island's caves are among its most fascinating natural treasures, offering a glimpse into a subterranean realm shaped over millions of years. These caves, formed by the relentless work of water and time, are as diverse as the landscapes above them. From vast underground chambers adorned with stalactites and stalagmites to narrow passages that echo with the whispers of ancient waters, Sardinia's caves captivate all who venture into their depths. Among them, Grotta di Nettuno stands as a crown jewel, but it is only one piece of a larger network of caverns that beckon explorers and nature enthusiasts alike. To step into these caves is to embark on a journey through time, where the earth tells its story in stone and silence.

Grotta di Nettuno, or Neptune's Grotto, is perhaps the most famous of Sardinia's caves and a must-see destination for visitors to the island. Located near Alghero on the northwestern coast, this spectacular sea cave is perched at the base of the dramatic Capo Caccia cliffs. The entrance to the cave can be reached by boat or via the Escala del Cabirol, a steep staircase of 654 steps carved into the cliffside. The approach alone is an unforgettable experience, offering panoramic views of the Mediterranean's shimmering waters and the rugged coastline. Once inside, Grotta di Nettuno reveals a breathtaking subterranean landscape that seems almost otherworldly.

The cave's main chamber is an awe-inspiring space, illuminated by soft lighting that highlights the intricate formations of stalactites and stalagmites. These mineral structures, formed over countless millennia by the slow drip of water, create an almost sculptural environment that feels like a natural cathedral. At the heart of the grotto lies the Lago Lamarmora, a vast underground saltwater lake that stretches nearly 120 meters in length. Its still, glassy surface reflects the surrounding formations, amplifying their beauty and creating a sense of serenity and wonder. Guided tours through Grotta di Nettuno provide insights into its geology, history, and legends, adding depth to the experience.

While Grotta di Nettuno is the most famous, Sardinia's caves extend far beyond its limestone chambers. In the eastern part of the island, the Supramonte region boasts an extensive network of caves that are equally captivating. Grotta del Bue Marino, named after the Mediterranean monk seal that once inhabited its waters, is a remarkable example. This cave, located near Cala Gonone, is accessible by boat and offers a stunning combination of natural beauty and archaeological significance. The cave's galleries feature impressive stalactites and stalagmites, as well as ancient rock carvings attributed to the Nuragic civilization. These carvings, depicting human figures and animals, suggest that the cave held spiritual or ceremonial importance for Sardinia's early inhabitants.

Another Supramonte gem is Grotta di Ispinigoli, home to one of Europe's tallest stalagmites. This towering column, which rises 38 meters from the cave floor, is a testament to the immense power of nature and the passage of time. Ispinigoli is also known for its "Abyss of the Virgins," a vertical shaft that plunges over 60 meters into the earth and connects to a vast underground network of tunnels and chambers. The cave's haunting beauty and sense of mystery make it a favorite among adventurers and geologists alike.

For those seeking a more rugged and remote caving experience, Su Palu and Su Bentu in the Gola di Gorropu area offer unparalleled opportunities for exploration. These interconnected cave systems are among the longest in Italy, with over 35 kilometers of mapped passages. Navigating their twisting tunnels and subterranean rivers requires skill and preparation, but the rewards are immense. Inside, you'll find intricate formations, hidden waterfalls, and chambers that seem untouched by time. Su Palu and Su Bentu epitomize the raw, untamed beauty of Sardinia's underground world, challenging even the most experienced cavers while offering glimpses of nature's artistry at its most sublime.

Sardinia's caves are not just geological marvels; they are also windows into the island's history and prehistory. Many caves have yielded archaeological discoveries that shed light on the lives of ancient peoples who sought shelter or conducted rituals in these hidden spaces. Grotta di San Giovanni, located near Domusnovas in southwestern Sardinia, is a notable example. This cave, one of the longest natural tunnels in the world, was used as a passageway for centuries and features evidence of human activity dating back to prehistoric times. Today, it is accessible by foot or bike, allowing visitors to experience its unique combination of natural and cultural significance.

Equally intriguing is the Grotta Verde near Alghero, which contains Neolithic carvings and artifacts. These findings suggest that the cave was used as a sacred site, possibly for fertility rituals or ceremonies honoring the cycles of nature. The interplay between the natural formations and the human marks left within them creates a powerful sense of connection across time, reminding us of the enduring relationship between humanity and the earth.

Exploring Sardinia's caves requires preparation and respect for the delicate environments they represent. Many caves are protected as natural or archaeological sites, and access may be restricted to guided tours to ensure their preservation. Proper footwear, clothing, and equipment are essential, particularly for more challenging caves that involve climbing, crawling, or wading through water. It's also important to be mindful of the impact of human activity on these fragile ecosystems, from avoiding touching formations to carrying out all waste. By treading lightly, visitors can help ensure that Sardinia's caves remain pristine for future generations to discover and appreciate.

The allure of Sardinia's caves lies not only in their physical beauty but also in the sense of wonder and discovery they inspire. Each cave is a unique microcosm, shaped by the interplay of water, rock, and time. Whether you're marveling at the grandeur of Grotta di Nettuno, tracing the footsteps of ancient peoples in Grotta Verde, or venturing deep into the labyrinthine passages of Su Palu, Sardinia's caves offer experiences that are as diverse as they are unforgettable. To step into these underground worlds is to embark on a journey that transcends the ordinary, revealing the hidden depths of an island that continues to surprise and inspire.

Cycling the Island's Scenic Routes

Sardinia offers a unique opportunity for cyclists to explore its diverse landscapes, blending the thrill of the ride with breathtaking vistas, cultural landmarks, and a sense of freedom that only two wheels can provide. The island's cycling routes range from peaceful coastal paths to challenging mountainous ascents, making it a destination suitable for novices and seasoned riders alike. Cycling in Sardinia is more than just a physical activity; it's a way to connect with the island's natural beauty, uncover hidden gems, and immerse yourself in a culture that thrives in harmony with its surroundings. Whether you're pedaling alongside turquoise waters or winding through ancient villages, each route tells its own story, and the joy lies in discovering it with every turn of the wheel.

One of the most iconic cycling routes in Sardinia is the Strada Panoramica della Costa del Sud, a scenic coastal road in the island's southernmost region. Stretching from Chia to Teulada, this winding route hugs the coastline, offering stunning views of the Mediterranean Sea and the rugged cliffs that define this part of the island. The turquoise waters glimmer below as the road meanders past sandy beaches, wild coves, and jagged rock formations. The route is relatively gentle, making it accessible to cyclists of varying fitness levels, but it does feature stretches of rolling hills that add just the right amount of challenge. The sense of accomplishment as you crest each hill and see the horizon unfold before you is unmatched, and the occasional stop to dip your toes in the clear, refreshing sea makes the journey all the more rewarding.

For those seeking a more leisurely ride while soaking in Sardinia's cultural atmosphere, the Marmilla region in the island's southwest is an excellent choice. This area is characterized by gentle rolling hills, fertile plains, and charming villages that seem untouched by time. Starting in the small town of Barumini, cyclists can visit Su Nuraxi, a UNESCO World Heritage Site and one of Sardinia's most significant archaeological treasures. The ride through Marmilla combines history, nature, and local traditions, with opportunities to stop at local farms to sample fresh pecorino cheese or sip a glass of Cannonau wine. The pace here is unhurried, allowing riders to enjoy the simple pleasures of the Sardinian countryside.

The eastern coast of Sardinia offers a more rugged and adventurous cycling experience, particularly in the region of Ogliastra. Known as the "Wild Heart of Sardinia," Ogliastra boasts dramatic landscapes that challenge and inspire in equal measure. The route from Baunei to Cala Gonone is a prime example, taking cyclists through the Supramonte mountain range and along roads that cling to the cliffs above the Tyrrhenian Sea. The ascent is steep and demanding, but the views are nothing short of spectacular. On one side, the jagged limestone peaks of the Supramonte rise majestically, while on the other, the endless expanse of the sea stretches to the horizon. This is a ride for those who crave both physical exertion and the exhilaration of being surrounded by nature at its most untamed.

For cyclists who prefer off-road adventures, Sardinia offers a wealth of trails that traverse its forests, hills, and even archaeological sites. The area around Monte Arci in central Sardinia is particularly well-suited to mountain biking. Monte Arci, an extinct volcanic massif, is crisscrossed with trails that range from easy loops to technical descents. The terrain is varied, with sections of dense woodland, open meadows, and rocky outcrops. One of the highlights of cycling in this area is the chance to find pieces of obsidian, the volcanic glass that was once highly prized for making tools. The trails also lead to ancient nuraghi and domus de janas (prehistoric tombs), adding a layer of historical intrigue to the ride.

The island's northern regions, such as Gallura, offer yet another dimension to Sardinia's cycling appeal. Gallura is known for its granite landscapes, cork oak forests, and the famous Costa Smeralda, one of the most glamorous stretches of coastline in the Mediterranean. A popular route in this area is the ride from Olbia to Porto Cervo, passing through small villages and rolling hills before reaching the glittering beaches and luxury resorts of the Costa Smeralda. While this route is relatively easy in terms of elevation, the allure lies in its contrasts: from quiet rural roads to the opulent charm of Porto Cervo, the journey encapsulates the diverse character of Sardinia.

No discussion of cycling in Sardinia would be complete without mentioning the island's mountainous interior, particularly the Gennargentu massif. This area is a playground for cyclists who relish the challenge of steep climbs and thrilling descents. The ride to Punta La Marmora, Sardinia's highest peak, is a test of endurance and determination, but the rewards are immense. The road winds through a landscape of alpine meadows, ancient forests, and sweeping valleys, culminating in panoramic views that take in nearly the entire island. The sense of achievement upon reaching the summit is unparalleled, and the descent, with its hairpin turns and exhilarating speeds, is pure adrenaline.

Cycling in Sardinia is not just about the routes; it's also about the connections you make along the way. The island's warm and welcoming locals often greet cyclists with a wave or a smile, and many small towns and villages have embraced cycling tourism, offering bike-friendly accommodations and services. Stopping at a roadside café for an espresso or a plate of malloreddus pasta provides not only sustenance but also an opportunity to experience Sardinia's renowned hospitality. These moments of connection remind you that cycling here is as much about the people as it is about the places.

The island's cycling infrastructure has improved significantly in recent years, with well-maintained roads, dedicated bike paths, and clear signage on many routes. However, it's still important to plan your rides carefully, especially in more remote areas where facilities may be limited. Carrying sufficient water, snacks, and a basic repair kit is essential, as is wearing appropriate clothing for Sardinia's often unpredictable weather. Cyclists should also be aware of local traffic laws and customs, particularly when riding on narrow rural roads shared with cars and tractors.

For those who want to explore Sardinia on two wheels without the hassle of planning every detail, guided cycling tours are an excellent option. These tours cater to a range of abilities and interests, from leisurely rides through vineyards to challenging multi-day expeditions across the island. Guided tours often include support vehicles, luggage transport, and knowledgeable guides who can provide insights into Sardinia's history, culture, and natural environment. Whether you choose to join a tour or go it alone, the freedom and sense of adventure that come with cycling in Sardinia are unmatched.

The rhythm of pedaling through Sardinia's landscapes allows you to experience the island in a way that is both intimate and exhilarating. The wind on your face, the scent of wildflowers, the sound of the sea crashing against the cliffs—all of these sensations come together to create a journey that is as much about the senses as it is about the miles. Each route, whether coastal or mountainous, tells a story of the island's natural beauty and cultural richness. Cycling in Sardinia is not just a physical activity; it's an exploration, an adventure, and a celebration of a land that reveals its secrets to those willing to ride a little further and climb a little higher.

Boat Tours and Sailing Adventures

Sardinia's coastline, stretching over 1,800 kilometers, is a marvel of natural beauty that is best experienced from the water. Its jagged cliffs, hidden coves, pristine beaches, and turquoise waters create a seascape so captivating that it almost demands to be explored by boat. Whether you're drawn to the idea of leisurely sailing along the coast, hopping between islands, or discovering secluded spots that can only be reached by sea, Sardinia offers a wealth of opportunities for boat tours and sailing adventures. These experiences not only provide an unforgettable perspective of the island but also immerse you in the rhythm of the Mediterranean, where the interplay of wind, waves, and sunlight creates a sense of freedom and connection with nature.

The Maddalena Archipelago, located off Sardinia's northeastern coast, is one of the most popular destinations for boat tours and a paradise for sailing enthusiasts. This cluster of seven main islands and numerous smaller islets is part of a protected national park, ensuring that its crystal-clear waters and unspoiled landscapes remain pristine. Setting sail from the nearby town of Palau, visitors can embark on a day-long excursion that takes them through this breathtaking marine haven. The journey typically includes stops at iconic spots like Spiaggia Rosa on Budelli Island, known for its unique pink sand, and the tranquil lagoons of Spargi and Santa Maria. The experience of anchoring in a sheltered bay, diving into the warm, translucent waters, and swimming alongside schools of fish is one that stays with you long after you've returned to shore.

For those seeking a more intimate connection with Sardinia's coastline, chartering a sailboat or joining a small-group sailing tour offers a unique sense of adventure and tranquility. Sailing along the Costa Smeralda, with its glamorous atmosphere and emerald-green waters, is an experience that combines natural beauty with a touch of sophistication. As the boat glides past luxurious villas and exclusive beach clubs, it's easy to understand why this stretch of coastline is a favorite among the global elite. Yet, beyond the glitz, the Costa Smeralda also reveals secluded coves and uninhabited islands that feel like hidden treasures. Spending a day or even a week on a sailboat allows you to escape the crowds, follow the rhythm of the wind, and wake up each morning to a new horizon.

The Gulf of Orosei, on Sardinia's eastern coast, offers a dramatically different but equally stunning setting for boat tours. Here, towering limestone cliffs plunge into the sea, creating a coastline that is wild, rugged, and awe-inspiring. Boat excursions departing from Cala Gonone take visitors to some of the most spectacular beaches in the Mediterranean, including Cala Luna, Cala Mariolu, and Cala Goloritzé. These beaches, accessible only by boat or on foot, are renowned for their powdery white sand and crystalline waters. Along the way, the boat weaves past hidden caves and grottos, such as the Grotta del Bue Marino, once a refuge for the endangered Mediterranean monk seal. Exploring these caves, with their intricate rock formations and shimmering underground lakes, adds a sense of mystery and wonder to the journey.

For a more immersive experience, multi-day sailing trips around Sardinia's coast offer the chance to explore the island at a leisurely pace, allowing you to delve deeper into its natural and cultural treasures. These voyages often include stops at lesser-known destinations, such as the island of Asinara in the northwest. Once a penal colony and now a national park, Asinara is a place of haunting beauty and ecological importance. Sailing to Asinara provides the opportunity to explore its pristine beaches, hike its rugged trails, and encounter wildlife such as wild donkeys and rare bird species.

The southwestern coast of Sardinia, with its dramatic cliffs and ancient ruins, is another compelling destination for sailing adventures. The area around the island of San Pietro, home to the charming town of Carloforte, is particularly enchanting. San Pietro's volcanic origins are evident in its rugged coastline, which features sea stacks, caves, and natural pools. Sailing around the island reveals hidden gems like Cala Vinagra and La Caletta, where you can anchor and enjoy the solitude of these remote spots. Carloforte, with its distinctive Ligurian heritage, offers a delightful contrast to the natural surroundings, with its colorful houses, vibrant piazzas, and renowned tuna dishes.

For those new to sailing or seeking a more guided experience, joining an organized boat tour or hiring a skipper is an excellent way to explore Sardinia's waters. Many tours are tailored to specific interests, such as snorkeling, diving, or even dolphin watching. The waters around Sardinia are teeming with marine life, and a guided tour can enhance your understanding and appreciation of the underwater world. Snorkeling in the Marine Protected Area of Capo Carbonara, near Villasimius, offers the chance to encounter vibrant coral reefs, octopuses, and schools of colorful fish. Meanwhile, dolphin-watching tours around the Gulf of Alghero provide an unforgettable opportunity to observe these playful creatures in their natural habitat.

One of the joys of exploring Sardinia by boat is the sense of spontaneity and discovery that comes with it. Unlike a fixed itinerary on land, a day on the water is shaped by the whims of the wind and the sea. A hidden cove glimpsed from the deck, a pod of dolphins leaping in the distance, or the chance to swim in a secluded bay—all of these moments add a sense of magic to the experience. Even the act of sailing itself, feeling the boat respond to the wind and the waves, becomes a source of exhilaration and connection with the elements.

Practical considerations are essential for ensuring a safe and enjoyable boat or sailing adventure in Sardinia. The island's weather and sea conditions can vary, particularly during the

Mistral winds that sweep in from the northwest. Checking the forecast and consulting with local experts before setting out is crucial. Proper equipment, including life jackets, navigation tools, and sufficient provisions, is also a must, especially for longer trips or remote areas with limited facilities. Many sailing charters and tours provide all necessary equipment and guidance, making it easier for beginners to enjoy the experience without worry.

Exploring Sardinia by boat also opens up opportunities to engage with its maritime traditions and cuisine. Local fishermen, who have plied these waters for generations, often share their knowledge and stories with visitors. Sampling freshly caught seafood, such as grilled fish, bottarga, or fregola with clams, adds a culinary dimension to the adventure. In coastal towns and villages, the connection between the sea and daily life is evident, from the bustling fish markets to the festivals that celebrate Sardinia's seafaring heritage.

The memories made on a boat tour or sailing trip in Sardinia linger long after you've returned to land. The feeling of the sun on your skin, the sound of the waves lapping against the hull, and the sight of the island's dramatic landscapes from the water create a sensory experience that stays with you. Beyond the beauty and adventure, there is a deeper sense of appreciation for the island's natural wonders and the rhythms of life that revolve around the sea. Sardinia's waters invite exploration, promising both discovery and a profound connection to a world that is as timeless as it is extraordinary.

Wildlife and Birdwatching in Sardinia

Sardinia's unique geography and mild Mediterranean climate have cultivated a haven for wildlife, attracting an extraordinary variety of species that thrive in the island's diverse ecosystems. From the rugged mountains of Gennargentu to the tranquil wetlands of Cabras, the island presents a mosaic of habitats that are home to rare animals, endemic plants, and a dazzling array of birdlife. For nature enthusiasts, Sardinia offers an unparalleled opportunity to observe its wild inhabitants in their natural environment, whether you're tracking elusive mammals, marveling at the vibrancy of its bird species, or simply appreciating the delicate balance of its ecosystems. The island's remoteness and relatively low human population density have allowed it to maintain an ecological richness that feels increasingly rare in today's world.

The Sardinian deer, or *Cervus elaphus corsicanus*, is one of the island's most iconic species. Found only in Sardinia and Corsica, this subspecies of red deer is smaller and stockier than its mainland counterparts, an adaptation to the island's rugged terrain. These majestic animals are most often spotted in the dense forests of the southwest, particularly in the Monte Arcosu Nature Reserve. Early mornings and evenings are the best times to catch sight of them, especially during the autumn mating season when males emit their distinctive calls. With their striking antlers and cautious movements, encountering Sardinian deer in the wild is a moment that stirs a deep appreciation for the island's untamed beauty.

The mouflon, an ancient wild sheep species, is another emblematic inhabitant of Sardinia's wilderness. Renowned for their agility and ability to navigate steep cliffs, mouflons can often be found in the mountainous regions of Supramonte and Gennargentu. Their reddish-brown coats and curved horns make them instantly recognizable, and their elusive nature adds an element of excitement to any wildlife-watching excursion. Observing a small herd perched precariously on a rocky outcrop is a reminder of the resilience and adaptability of Sardinia's fauna.

The wetlands and lagoons scattered across the island provide a stark contrast to the rugged interior, yet they are no less vital to Sardinia's biodiversity. These areas, including the Molentargius-Saline Regional Park near Cagliari and the Stagno di Cabras on the western coast, are sanctuaries for a wide range of bird species. Flamingos are arguably the stars of these wetlands, their pink feathers a striking contrast against the shimmering waters. Sardinia is one of the most important breeding sites for flamingos in the Mediterranean, and seeing them gather in large flocks is a spectacle that draws birdwatchers from around the world.

Beyond the wetlands, Sardinia's coastal cliffs and islands are a haven for seabirds. The island of Asinara, now a national park, is a particularly rich birdwatching destination. Here, you might encounter Audouin's gull, a rare species that nests along the Mediterranean coast, as well as the Mediterranean shag and the Cory's shearwater. These seabirds rely on the island's rugged coastline and surrounding waters, which remain largely undisturbed, for nesting and feeding. Observing them as they soar above the waves or return to their rocky perches is a humbling reminder of the intricate connections between land and sea.

The golden eagle is a symbol of the island's wild heart, reigning over Sardinia's skies with an undeniable majesty.

159

These raptors are most often seen in the Gennargentu and Supramonte mountain ranges, where they hunt small mammals and birds. Spotting a golden eagle in flight, its massive wingspan silhouetted against the sky, is a moment of awe that stays with you long after the encounter. Sardinia is also home to other birds of prey, such as the peregrine falcon and the griffon vulture, the latter of which has been the focus of conservation efforts to ensure its continued survival on the island.

Endemic species are among Sardinia's most fascinating residents, having evolved in isolation over thousands of years. The Sardinian newt, for example, is found only on the island and in a few nearby locations. This small, amphibious creature inhabits freshwater springs and ponds, and while it may not be as immediately striking as a golden eagle or a flamingo, its presence speaks to the island's unique ecological history. Similarly, the Sardinian brook salamander is another endemic amphibian that contributes to the island's rich biodiversity.

Reptiles, too, find a home in Sardinia's varied landscapes. The Hermann's tortoise, considered a symbol of longevity, can often be seen basking in the sun in the island's scrublands and forests. The Tyrrhenian wall lizard, with its vivid green coloration, is another highlight for those with an eye for smaller creatures. Sardinia's reptilian inhabitants are a reminder that every layer of its ecosystems, from the forest canopy to the forest floor, is teeming with life.

The flora of Sardinia complements its wildlife, creating habitats that sustain its diverse inhabitants. Cork oak forests, which thrive in the island's Mediterranean climate, provide shelter for birds and mammals while supporting a traditional industry that has shaped local culture for centuries. The

Mediterranean maquis, a dense shrubland of aromatic herbs and plants, is another defining feature of the landscape. This habitat is home to countless insects and small animals, as well as being a source of food and shelter for larger species. The interplay between Sardinia's flora and fauna is a testament to the delicate balance of its ecosystems.

Conservation efforts play a crucial role in preserving Sardinia's natural heritage. National parks, reserves, and protected areas are vital for safeguarding habitats and species, particularly in the face of threats such as habitat loss and climate change. Initiatives like the reintroduction of the griffon vulture to the island demonstrate the importance of active conservation in maintaining biodiversity. Visitors to Sardinia can contribute to these efforts by respecting the natural environment, following guidelines in protected areas, and supporting local conservation organizations.

Observing wildlife in Sardinia is as much about patience and respect as it is about opportunity. The island's creatures are not confined to enclosures or schedules; they move according to their own rhythms, often requiring keen observation and quiet persistence to spot. Early mornings and late afternoons are typically the best times for wildlife watching, as many animals are most active during these cooler hours. Bringing binoculars, a field guide, and a sense of curiosity enhances the experience, allowing you to fully engage with the natural world around you.

The sounds of Sardinia's wildlife are as evocative as its sights. The call of a Sardinian warbler, the rustle of a lizard in the underbrush, or the distant cry of an eagle echoing through the mountains create an auditory tapestry that immerses you in the island's wild spaces. These moments, often fleeting and subtle, are what make wildlife watching in Sardinia so rewarding. They remind you that you are a guest in a world that has existed long before you arrived and will continue long after you've left.

Sardinia's wildlife and birdwatching opportunities offer a deeper connection to the island, revealing the intricacies of its ecosystems and the resilience of its inhabitants. Whether you're tracking mouflons in the mountains, marveling at flamingos in the wetlands, or watching seabirds glide over the waves, each encounter is a reminder of the island's untamed spirit. Sardinia invites you to step into its wild heart, where every sighting, sound, and moment of stillness becomes part of a larger story—one that speaks to the beauty and fragility of the natural world.

CHAPTER 6: SARDINIAN CUISINE AND LOCAL FLAVORS

Traditional Sardinian Dishes You Must Try

Sardinia's culinary heritage is as rich and diverse as the island itself, shaped by centuries of tradition, geography, and the interplay of cultures that have left their mark on this Mediterranean jewel. Its cuisine is rooted in simplicity, with a focus on high-quality, locally sourced ingredients that reflect the island's agricultural and pastoral traditions. From hearty bread and cheeses to delicate seafood dishes, each bite tells a story of Sardinia's landscapes, its people, and their enduring connection to the land and sea. Exploring traditional Sardinian dishes is not just a journey of flavors—it's a deep dive into the heart of the island's identity, where every dish brings you closer to understanding its history and way of life.

Pane carasau, often referred to as Sardinian flatbread, is a cornerstone of the island's cuisine and a testament to its pastoral roots. This thin, crisp bread originated as a staple for shepherds who needed a durable, long-lasting food to sustain them during their time in the mountains. Its preparation is an art form, involving a double baking process that gives it its signature texture and ability to stay fresh for weeks. Pane carasau is versatile, enjoyed plain, drizzled with olive oil, or transformed into pane frattau, a dish where layers of the bread are softened with broth, topped with tomato sauce, and crowned with a poached egg. The simplicity of pane carasau belies its significance, as it embodies the resourcefulness and ingenuity of Sardinian cuisine.

Another essential element of Sardinian gastronomy is its cheese, with pecorino sardo standing out as a true icon. Made from sheep's milk, pecorino sardo is produced in varying stages of aging, from young and mild to mature and intensely flavored. Its production is deeply tied to the island's pastoral tradition, where sheep farming has been a way of life for generations. The cheese is often enjoyed on its own, paired with local honey for a blend of savory and sweet, or grated over pasta dishes to enhance their richness. For the adventurous, there is also casu marzu, a controversial and unique cheese that is fermented with the help of fly larvae. While not for the faint of heart, casu marzu is a symbol of Sardinia's unapologetically bold approach to food and a reminder of the island's deep-rooted culinary traditions.

Malloreddus, often called Sardinian gnocchi, is a beloved pasta dish that captures the essence of the island's home-cooked meals. These small, ridged pasta shapes are made with semolina flour and water, their grooves perfect for holding rich sauces. The most traditional preparation is malloreddus alla campidanese, a hearty dish featuring a tomato-based sauce flavored with saffron, sausage, and pecorino cheese. The addition of saffron, grown in the Campidano plain, adds a touch of luxury and a reminder of Sardinia's ties to ancient trade routes. To sit down to a plate of malloreddus is to experience the warmth and comfort of Sardinian hospitality at its finest.

Culurgiones, a type of filled pasta, are more than just a dish— they are a representation of Sardinian craftsmanship and cultural pride. These dumpling-like creations are typically stuffed with a mixture of potatoes, pecorino cheese, and mint, then sealed with a distinctive braided pattern that resembles an ear of wheat. This intricate closure, known as "sa spighitta," is both a practical and decorative element that showcases the skill of the cook. Traditionally prepared during special occasions or as an offering of gratitude, culurgiones are often served with a simple tomato sauce or butter and sage, allowing their delicate flavors to shine. They reflect the island's agricultural heritage and the importance of community in its culinary traditions.

The bounty of Sardinia's coastline is evident in its seafood dishes, which feature prominently in the island's cuisine. Fregola con arselle is a standout, combining fregola—a type of toasted semolina pasta resembling small beads—with clams in a light, flavorful broth. The nuttiness of the fregola complements the briny sweetness of the clams, creating a dish that is both comforting and sophisticated. Bottarga, often referred to as the "gold of Sardinia," is another seafood delicacy that showcases the island's fishing heritage. Made from cured mullet roe, bottarga is typically shaved over pasta or served in thin slices with olive oil and lemon. Its intense, salty flavor is a testament to the islanders' resourcefulness in preserving the fruits of the sea.

Porceddu, or roast suckling pig, is perhaps the most iconic dish of Sardinia's land-based cuisine. This celebration of simplicity and flavor involves slow-roasting a whole pig over a wood fire, often seasoned with little more than salt, myrtle, and rosemary. The result is a tender, succulent meat with crispy, golden skin that is a highlight of any traditional Sardinian feast. Porceddu is often served during festivals, weddings, and other special occasions, where it becomes the centerpiece of a communal meal. It reflects the island's deep

166

respect for its agricultural roots and the importance of sharing food as a way of bringing people together.

Zuppa gallurese, a dish from the Gallura region in northern Sardinia, is a rustic and hearty creation that blurs the line between soup and casserole. Made with layers of stale bread, pecorino cheese, and a rich meat broth, it is baked until golden and bubbling. Despite its humble ingredients, zuppa gallurese is a dish of great depth and comfort, embodying the resourcefulness of Sardinian cooking. It is often served during family gatherings and celebrations, where its warm, satisfying nature makes it a favorite among guests.

Desserts in Sardinia are a testament to the island's love of simple, honest flavors. Seadas, perhaps the most famous, are large, cheese-filled pastries that are fried and drizzled with honey. The combination of the crispy pastry, the melted pecorino cheese, and the sweetness of the honey creates a dessert that is both indulgent and uniquely Sardinian. Amaretti, made with almonds, sugar, and egg whites, are another beloved treat, their chewy texture and nutty flavor making them perfect alongside a cup of coffee. Sardinia's desserts often reflect the island's agricultural bounty, from almonds and honey to citrus fruits and saffron.

To accompany these traditional dishes, Sardinia offers a selection of wines and spirits that complement its cuisine. Cannonau, a robust red wine, is perhaps the most famous, its bold flavors pairing beautifully with meats and cheeses. Vermentino, a crisp and aromatic white wine, is the perfect match for seafood dishes and lighter fare. Mirto, a liqueur made from myrtle berries, is often served as a digestif, its aromatic and slightly bitter notes providing a fitting end to a meal. These beverages are more than just drinks—they are an integral part of Sardinia's culinary experience, reflecting the island's terroir and the dedication of its winemakers and distillers.

Traditional Sardinian cuisine is a celebration of the island's history, geography, and way of life. Each dish, from the simplest flatbread to the most elaborate roast, tells a story of the land and the people who have cultivated it for generations. To taste Sardinia's food is to connect with its past and present, to savor not just flavors but the spirit of an island that has remained true to itself. The richness and authenticity of Sardinian cuisine make it an essential part of any journey to this extraordinary place, offering a feast for the senses and a window into its soul.

Sardinia's Famous Wines and Wineries

Sardinia's winemaking tradition is as ancient and storied as the island itself, its history interwoven with the cultures and peoples who have called this land home. The island's wines, shaped by its distinctive climate, soil, and grape varieties, stand as a testament to the resilience and creativity of Sardinian viticulture. With rolling vineyards that stretch across the land, from coastal plains to rugged hillsides, Sardinia offers a wine culture that is both unique and deeply rooted in its identity. Visiting its wineries and exploring its famous wines is not just a sensory journey but a gateway into the heart of the island's heritage, where every bottle tells its own story, shaped by the hands of those who craft it and the land that nurtures it.

Cannonau di Sardegna, perhaps the most iconic of Sardinian wines, is deeply connected to the island's identity and history.

Known elsewhere as Grenache, this red grape thrives in Sardinia's hot, dry climate, producing wines that are robust, full-bodied, and rich in character. Some believe the grape has been cultivated on the island for over 3,000 years, making it one of the world's oldest known varietals. Cannonau is celebrated for its deep ruby color, flavors of ripe berries, and hints of spice, with a structure that balances power and elegance. It is often aged in oak barrels to enhance its complexity, developing notes of vanilla, tobacco, and dried herbs. When paired with Sardinian dishes like porceddu or mature pecorino cheese, Cannonau becomes more than a drink; it transforms into a bridge between the island's culinary and viticultural traditions.

Vermentino di Gallura, a shining star among Sardinia's white wines, captures the essence of the island's northern region with its freshness and vibrancy. Grown primarily in the granitic soils of Gallura, this grape produces wines that are crisp, aromatic, and intensely flavorful, often with notes of citrus, green apple, and Mediterranean herbs. Vermentino di Gallura is the only Sardinian wine to hold the prestigious DOCG designation, a mark of its exceptional quality and regional significance. Its bright acidity and mineral undertones make it an ideal companion for seafood dishes, from fregola with clams to grilled seabass, as well as lighter fare like vegetable antipasti. Sipping a chilled glass of Vermentino on a warm Sardinian evening is an experience that encapsulates the island's sun-drenched allure and the craftsmanship of its winemakers.

Carignano del Sulcis, grown in Sardinia's southwestern region, tells a story of resilience and adaptation. This red varietal, known as Carignan in other parts of the world, thrives in the sandy, wind-swept soils of Sulcis, where the vines are often ungrafted due to the phylloxera-resistant nature of the terrain. The result is a wine that is deeply expressive, with flavors of dark cherries, plums, and earthy spices, complemented by velvety tannins and a hint of salinity from the nearby sea. Carignano del Sulcis is often crafted as a single varietal wine, but it also shines in blends, showcasing the versatility of the grape. Its bold, yet approachable character pairs beautifully with hearty dishes like lamb stew or grilled meats, making it a favorite among Sardinian wine enthusiasts and beyond.

Monica di Sardegna, a red wine with a softer profile, offers a glimpse into the island's diversity of styles. This varietal is known for its light to medium body, with flavors of red fruits, violets, and a touch of spice. Monica wines are often enjoyed young, their freshness and smooth tannins making them an easy-drinking option that pairs well with a variety of foods, from charcuterie to tomato-based pastas. Despite its lighter character, Monica di Sardegna holds an important place in the island's winemaking tradition, offering a contrast to the more intense and structured reds like Cannonau and Carignano.

The wines of Vernaccia di Oristano are a world apart, offering a unique glimpse into Sardinia's ancient winemaking techniques. Produced in the Oristano region on the island's western coast, this white wine is made from the Vernaccia grape and undergoes an oxidative aging process in partially filled barrels. The result is a complex, amber-hued wine with nutty, sherry-like characteristics and notes of dried fruits, almonds, and honey. Vernaccia di Oristano is often enjoyed as an aperitif or paired with Sardinian desserts like amaretti and seadas, its richness and depth providing a fitting balance to the sweetness of these treats. This wine is a reminder of the island's ability to innovate while preserving its traditions, creating something truly distinctive.

Exploring Sardinia's wineries offers an intimate look at the passion and dedication that define its winemaking culture. From small, family-run estates to larger, internationally acclaimed producers, each winery has its own story and approach. In the Gallura region, the Cantina del Vermentino stands out for its commitment to showcasing the potential of Vermentino di Gallura, producing wines that reflect the unique terroir of the area. Visitors to the winery can tour the vineyards, learn about the winemaking process, and enjoy guided tastings that highlight the elegance and complexity of their wines.

In the Sulcis area, Cantina Santadi is a must-visit for those interested in Carignano del Sulcis. This cooperative winery has gained international recognition for its ability to elevate this varietal, producing wines that are both accessible and age-worthy. Their Terre Brune, a Carignano-based blend, is a particular standout, praised for its depth and sophistication. A visit to Cantina Santadi offers not only the chance to taste these exceptional wines but also to learn about the history and culture of the Sulcis region, where winemaking has been a way of life for centuries.

Barbagia, in the heart of Sardinia, is home to some of the island's most traditional wineries, where Cannonau reigns supreme. Cantina Giuseppe Sedilesu, located in the village of Mamoiada, is renowned for its biodynamic approach and commitment to preserving the integrity of the Cannonau grape. Their wines, crafted with minimal intervention, offer a pure expression of the grape and the land. Visitors to the winery can experience the warmth of Sardinian hospitality while exploring the nuances of Cannonau through guided tastings and vineyard tours.

The island's wine festivals provide another avenue for discovering its viticultural treasures. Events like Calici di Stelle, held in various locations across Sardinia during the summer, invite wine lovers to sample local wines under the stars, accompanied by music, food, and a celebratory atmosphere. These festivals are a testament to the island's deep connection to its wines, where they are not just a product but a source of pride and identity.

Sardinia's unique climate and geography play a crucial role in shaping its wines. The island's Mediterranean climate, with hot, dry summers and mild, wet winters, creates ideal conditions for grape cultivation. The diverse soils, ranging from granite and limestone to sand and clay, contribute to the complexity and distinctiveness of the wines. Many vineyards are located near the coast, where the sea breeze moderates temperatures and adds a subtle salinity to the wines, while others are nestled in the island's interior, where altitude and temperature variation enhance the grapes' aromatic qualities.

Sustainability is becoming an increasingly important focus for Sardinian winemakers, many of whom are adopting organic and biodynamic practices to protect the island's environment and ensure the health of their vineyards for future generations. These practices not only benefit the land but also result in wines that are a more authentic expression of their terroir. By prioritizing sustainability, Sardinia's wineries are preserving not just their vines but the cultural and natural heritage that makes their wines so special.

The experience of tasting Sardinian wine on the island itself is unparalleled, as it connects you to the land, the people, and the traditions that define it. Each sip carries the essence of Sardinia's sunlit vineyards, its coastal breezes, and the care of its winemakers. Whether you are savoring a glass of Cannonau alongside a plate of roasted meats, enjoying the crispness of Vermentino with fresh seafood, or marveling at the complexity of Vernaccia di Oristano, Sardinian wines offer a journey of discovery that lingers long after the last drop. They are not just beverages but a celebration of the island's spirit, its ability to endure, and its timeless connection to the art of winemaking.

The Art of Making Pecorino Cheese

The art of making pecorino cheese in Sardinia is a tradition that has been perfected over centuries, rooted in the island's pastoral culture and its relationship with its most iconic animal—the sheep. Sardinia is home to more sheep than people, and this abundance has made sheep's milk the cornerstone of its cheesemaking heritage. Pecorino, derived from the Italian word *pecora*, meaning sheep, is more than just a cheese here; it is a symbol of Sardinian identity and a product that reflects the island's rugged landscapes, its dry Mediterranean climate, and the dedication of its shepherds and artisans. Every wheel of pecorino carries with it the story of Sardinia's history, its people, and the harmonious balance they have maintained with nature.

The process of making pecorino cheese begins with the milk, which is collected from Sardinia's native sheep breeds, primarily the Sardinian breed known for its high-quality milk. The sheep graze freely on the island's hills and pastures, feeding on a variety of herbs, wildflowers, and grasses that lend their subtle flavors to the milk. This connection between the sheep's diet and the cheese's flavor is one of the defining characteristics of Sardinian pecorino. The milk is collected fresh, typically twice a day, ensuring that it retains its natural richness and freshness. Timing is critical, as the cheesemaking process often begins within hours of milking to preserve the milk's delicate qualities.

Once the milk is brought to the cheesemaking facility, it is typically heated to a specific temperature, depending on the desired type of pecorino. Traditional pecorino makers often rely on the use of natural rennet, extracted from the stomach lining of young lambs, to curdle the milk. This step is both a nod to tradition and a practice that enhances the cheese's distinctive flavor profile. The milk is stirred gently as the rennet is added, and within minutes, it begins to coagulate into curds. This transformation is both scientific and magical, a moment when the liquid milk takes its first step toward becoming cheese.

The curds are then carefully cut into small pieces, a step that determines the texture of the final product. Larger curds typically result in softer cheeses, while smaller curds yield harder, aged varieties. Sardinian cheesemakers use special tools, often wooden or metal knives, to perform this task with precision. The cut curds are stirred and sometimes gently heated to release whey, the liquid byproduct of the process. This stage requires an experienced hand, as overworking or underworking the curds can affect the consistency and flavor of the cheese.

Once the desired texture is achieved, the curds are transferred into molds, where they are pressed to remove additional whey and shape the cheese. Traditional pecorino molds are often lined with woven patterns that leave an imprint on the cheese's rind, adding an artisanal touch to its appearance. The pressing process can last several hours, during which the curds are flipped and pressed multiple times to ensure an even shape and consistency. The resulting cheese wheels are then removed from the molds and placed in a brine solution, where they absorb salt that enhances their flavor and acts as a natural preservative.

Aging, or maturation, is where pecorino truly develops its character. Sardinian pecorino can be aged for as little as a few weeks or as long as several years, with each stage offering a unique flavor and texture. Fresh pecorino, known as pecorino fresco, is soft, creamy, and mild, with a milky sweetness that pairs beautifully with honey or fresh fruit. Aged pecorino, or pecorino stagionato, is firmer and more intense, with nutty, tangy flavors that deepen over time. The aging process takes place in carefully controlled environments, often traditional cellars or caves, where temperature and humidity are closely monitored. During this time, the cheese is periodically turned and cleaned to ensure even aging and to develop its natural rind.

One of the most remarkable aspects of Sardinian pecorino is the diversity of its variations, each reflecting the specific techniques and traditions of the region where it is made. Pecorino Sardo, protected under the European Union's PDO (Protected Designation of Origin) label, is perhaps the most famous. It comes in two main varieties: dolce (sweet) and maturo (mature). Pecorino Sardo Dolce is a younger cheese, aged for just 20 to 60 days, with a soft texture and mild flavor. Pecorino Sardo Maturo, aged for at least 120 days, is more robust, with a firm texture and a complex, savory taste.

Another standout is Fiore Sardo, a traditional smoked pecorino that also holds PDO status. This cheese is made using raw sheep's milk and is often smoked over wood fires, a practice that dates back to ancient times when shepherds used smoke to preserve their cheese. The result is a cheese with a firm, crumbly texture and a rich, smoky flavor that pairs exceptionally well with rustic bread and robust red wines. Fiore Sardo is often produced in small batches by family-run farms, preserving its artisanal quality and connection to Sardinian heritage.

The most controversial and unique variation of pecorino is casu marzu, literally "rotten cheese." This highly unusual cheese is intentionally fermented with the help of fly larvae, which break down the fats and create an intensely soft, almost liquid interior. While illegal in some places due to health concerns, casu marzu is a cultural icon in Sardinia, often served during special occasions. Its pungent aroma and strong flavor are not for everyone, but for those who dare to try it, casu marzu represents the bold and unapologetic spirit of Sardinian cuisine.

Pecorino cheese is more than just food in Sardinia; it is a way of life. Shepherds, who have been the custodians of this tradition for generations, play a central role in the island's culture. Their knowledge of animal husbandry, their connection to the land, and their dedication to the craft are what make Sardinian pecorino so special. Many shepherds still follow age-old practices, such as moving their flocks to different pastures with the changing seasons, ensuring that the sheep have access to the freshest and most diverse forage.

Visitors to Sardinia can experience the art of pecorino cheesemaking firsthand through farm tours and workshops offered by local producers. These experiences provide a unique opportunity to witness every step of the process, from milking the sheep to tasting the finished product. Tasting pecorino on the island itself, paired with Sardinian wines, honey, or traditional flatbreads like pane carasau, offers a sensory connection to the land and its people that cannot be replicated elsewhere.

The global appreciation for Sardinian pecorino continues to grow, with the cheese finding its way onto plates and into markets far beyond the island's shores. Yet, despite its international recognition, pecorino remains deeply tied to Sardinia's identity. Each wheel of cheese is a tribute to the island's past, a product of its present, and a promise for its future. It is a reminder that even in a rapidly changing world, some traditions are worth preserving, not just for their flavors but for the stories they tell and the connections they foster. Sardinian pecorino is not just a cheese; it is a legacy, a symbol of the island's enduring spirit and its timeless art of making something extraordinary from the simplest of ingredients.

Seafood Delights and Coastal Cuisine

The coastal waters surrounding Sardinia are among the most pristine in the Mediterranean, and they are teeming with marine life that has shaped the island's culinary traditions for centuries. Sardinian seafood cuisine is a celebration of the ocean's bounty, blending simplicity and bold flavors to create dishes that are as vibrant as the island itself. From succulent shellfish to delicately grilled fish, the coastal cuisine of Sardinia is deeply rooted in the rhythms of the sea and the expertise of the fishermen who have passed down their knowledge through generations. It is impossible to experience the essence of Sardinia without indulging in its seafood, which reflects the island's connection to its waters and the enduring traditions of its coastal communities.

Fregola con arselle is a quintessential Sardinian seafood dish that highlights the island's ingenuity in creating simple yet unforgettable flavors. Fregola, a type of hand-rolled pasta resembling tiny beads, is toasted to give it a nutty flavor and a slightly firm texture. This pasta is then combined with arselle, small clams harvested from the shallow lagoons and coastal waters of Sardinia. The dish is typically prepared with a light broth of garlic, olive oil, white wine, and parsley, allowing the natural brininess of the clams to shine through. The beauty of fregola con arselle lies in its balance of textures and flavors— each bite offers the delicate chew of the fregola, the tender sweetness of the clams, and the aromatic depth of its simple seasoning. It is a dish that speaks to the heart of Sardinian cooking, where the quality of the ingredients is paramount and the preparation respects their natural essence.

Bottarga, often referred to as Sardinia's "gold of the sea," is another iconic element of the island's seafood repertoire. Made from the salted and cured roe of mullet or tuna, bottarga is a delicacy that embodies the islanders' resourcefulness and skill in preservation. The roe sacs are carefully cleaned, salted, and pressed before being left to air-dry, resulting in a firm, amber-colored product with an intense, briny flavor. Bottarga is typically shaved or grated over dishes to add a burst of umami, and it is most commonly served with pasta, olive oil, and a sprinkling of lemon zest. This simple preparation allows the bottarga's bold taste to take center stage, transforming even the most basic ingredients into a gourmet experience.

Beyond its culinary significance, bottarga also holds cultural importance, serving as a symbol of Sardinia's deep ties to its fishing heritage and its ability to create luxury from the humblest of resources.

The island's coastline is dotted with small fishing villages, each with its own specialties and traditions that contribute to Sardinia's diverse seafood offerings. In the southwestern region, the town of Carloforte on the island of San Pietro is renowned for its tuna, particularly bluefin tuna, which has been a cornerstone of its economy and cuisine for centuries. The annual Girotonno festival celebrates this heritage with a showcase of tuna-based dishes, from carpaccio and tartare to stews and grilled fillets. One of the most beloved preparations is tonno alla carlofortina, a dish that combines fresh tuna with tomatoes, onions, and capers, creating a medley of flavors that is both hearty and refreshing. This dish exemplifies the Carloforte community's ability to honor its maritime roots while embracing the culinary influences of Ligurian settlers who arrived centuries ago.

Sea urchins, or ricci di mare, are a prized delicacy in Sardinia, their briny, slightly sweet roe offering a pure taste of the sea. Harvested during the cooler months when their flavor is at its peak, sea urchins are often enjoyed raw, scooped directly from the spiny shell and eaten with a slice of bread or a squeeze of lemon. For a more elaborate preparation, their roe is incorporated into pasta dishes, where it lends a creamy, luxurious texture and an intense oceanic flavor. Spaghetti ai ricci di mare is a standout example, combining the richness of the roe with the simplicity of garlic, olive oil, and a touch of chili. This dish captures the essence of Sardinian coastal cuisine—fresh, unpretentious, and deeply connected to the sea.

The variety of fish found in Sardinian waters is astounding, and these are often prepared with minimal embellishments to let their natural flavors shine. Orata (gilthead bream) and spigola (sea bass) are among the most popular choices, often grilled whole and served with little more than olive oil, lemon, and fresh herbs. The technique of grilling fish over an open flame, known as *alla brace*, is a time-honored tradition that highlights the islanders' respect for their ingredients. The fish is often accompanied by contorni, or side dishes, such as roasted potatoes or a simple salad of wild greens, creating a meal that is as satisfying as it is straightforward.

Sardinia's crustaceans also take center stage in its seafood cuisine, with lobster being a particular highlight. The spiny lobster, or aragosta, is especially prized and is often prepared in the traditional Alghero style, known as aragosta alla catalana. This dish features succulent lobster meat paired with a vibrant salad of tomatoes, onions, and olive oil, sometimes accented with a drizzle of vinegar. The simplicity of the preparation allows the natural sweetness of the lobster to shine, while the fresh vegetables provide a crisp, tangy contrast. Aragosta alla catalana is a dish that showcases Sardinia's ability to elevate its ingredients with minimal intervention, creating a harmony of flavors that feels both luxurious and approachable.

Octopus, or polpo, is another staple of Sardinian coastal cuisine, its tender meat lending itself to a variety of preparations. Polpo alla diavola, or "devil-style" octopus, is a bold and flavorful dish that features octopus cooked in a spicy tomato sauce with garlic and chili. The slow-cooking process ensures the octopus remains tender while absorbing the rich flavors of the sauce. For a lighter option, insalata di polpo, or octopus salad, combines boiled octopus with potatoes, parsley, and olive oil, resulting in a dish that is as refreshing as it is satisfying. These preparations highlight the versatility of octopus and its ability to adapt to both rustic and refined interpretations.

The island's seafood is often paired with Sardinia's exceptional wines, which enhance the dining experience and reflect the island's terroir. Vermentino di Gallura, with its crisp acidity and citrus notes, is a natural companion for seafood dishes, cutting through the richness of lobster or complementing the brininess of clams. Cannonau, a bold and fruity red, pairs surprisingly well with heartier seafood preparations like tuna or octopus in tomato-based sauces. These pairings are a testament to the island's holistic approach to food and drink, where each element is carefully considered to create a cohesive and memorable experience.

Sardinia's coastal cuisine is not just about the dishes themselves but also about the traditions and stories that surround them. Many recipes have been passed down through families, evolving over time while remaining true to their origins. Fishermen's markets, where the day's catch is displayed in all its glistening freshness, are a vital part of this culture, offering a glimpse into the island's intimate relationship with the sea. Even the act of dining on seafood is steeped in a sense of place, whether it's enjoying a leisurely meal at a seaside trattoria or savoring a simple picnic of bread and sea urchins on a rocky shore.

The flavors of Sardinian seafood cuisine are as varied and dynamic as the island's coastline, offering a sensory journey that captures the essence of life by the sea. Each dish, from the humble fregola con arselle to the indulgent aragosta alla catalana, is a reflection of the island's culinary philosophy: to honor its ingredients, its traditions, and its people. Sardinia invites you to taste its waters, to savor its coastal bounty, and to experience the deep connection between its cuisine and its identity. It is a place where the sea is not just a backdrop but a source of life, nourishment, and inspiration, shaping a cuisine that is as timeless as the waves that lap its shores.

Sweet Treats and Pastries of Sardinia

Sardinia's sweet treats and pastries are an irresistible part of the island's culinary heritage, a reflection of its history, culture, and the deep connection its people have with traditional recipes passed down through generations. These desserts, often tied to religious festivals, seasonal celebrations, and family gatherings, are a testament to Sardinia's ability to transform simple, local ingredients into works of art. From almond-based confections to honey-drizzled pastries, Sardinian sweets are as varied and unique as the island's landscapes. Every bite tells a story of craftsmanship, patience, and a love for preserving the tastes of the past while celebrating the joys of the present.

Seadas, arguably the most famous Sardinian dessert, is a perfect example of the island's ability to marry sweet and savory flavors into a harmonious whole. This large, golden pastry is made from a delicate dough of semolina and lard, filled with fresh pecorino cheese that softens as it is fried to perfection. Once removed from the sizzling oil, the seadas is generously drizzled with honey, often from local sources such as wildflower or bitter strawberry tree honey, adding a touch of sweetness that contrasts beautifully with the tangy, slightly salty cheese. Traditionally served warm, seadas is more than just a dessert; it is a celebration of Sardinia's pastoral roots, its beekeeping traditions, and its enduring love for simple, bold flavors. Each bite is a sensory journey, the crisp exterior giving way to the molten cheese center, all balanced by the aromatic sweetness of honey.

Amaretti, the soft, chewy almond cookies that are a staple in Sardinian households, have a texture and flavor that make them instantly recognizable. Made from a simple mixture of ground almonds, sugar, and egg whites, these cookies are as much about the quality of the almonds as they are about the care taken in their preparation. Sardinia's almonds, grown in the island's fertile soil and kissed by the Mediterranean sun, lend a richness and depth of flavor to amaretti that is unparalleled. The cookies are often flavored with a hint of bitter almond extract, which adds a slight, aromatic edge that balances their sweetness. Amaretti are versatile, equally at home alongside a cup of coffee, as a light dessert, or even as a gift wrapped in colorful tissue paper. Their simplicity belies their significance in Sardinian culture, where they are a symbol of hospitality and warmth.

Papassini, traditional Sardinian biscuits often associated with the feast of All Saints, are another testament to the island's knack for combining bold ingredients in creative ways. These cookies are typically made with a rich dough of flour, sugar, and lard or butter, studded with raisins, walnuts, and orange zest. Once baked to a golden hue, they are often glazed with a thin layer of icing, which adds both sweetness and an inviting sheen. Papassini are deeply tied to Sardinian traditions, particularly during the autumn months, when they are prepared to honor loved ones who have passed. Their intricate flavors and textures, with the crunch of nuts and the chewiness of raisins, make them a favorite among Sardinians and visitors alike. Eating a papassino is like taking a bite of Sardinia's history, its layers of influence, and its enduring connection to family and community.

Torrone, or nougat, is a sweet treat that showcases Sardinia's rich honey production and the island's love for almonds and walnuts. While nougat is found in many Mediterranean regions, Sardinian torrone is unique for its texture and flavor, which are achieved through the use of local honey as the primary sweetener. The honey is heated and whipped with egg whites until it becomes light and airy, then combined with toasted nuts and molded into bars or blocks. In towns like Tonara, which is famous for its torrone, this delicacy is often sold at festivals and fairs, where you can watch artisans prepare it in large copper pots over open flames. Sardinian torrone is soft and chewy, with a subtle floral sweetness from the honey and a satisfying crunch from the nuts. It is a dessert that speaks to the island's natural abundance and its tradition of honoring that abundance through skilled craftsmanship.

Gueffus, small almond-based confections, are another highlight of Sardinian sweets, their simplicity masking the precision required to make them just right. These bite-sized treats are made by blending ground almonds with sugar and a hint of citrus zest, then rolling the mixture into balls and wrapping them in colorful tissue paper. Gueffus are often given as gifts during weddings, baptisms, or other celebrations, their vibrant wrappings adding a festive touch to any occasion. The texture of gueffus is soft and slightly crumbly, with a delicate sweetness that makes them almost addictive. They are a reminder of Sardinia's love for almonds and its ability to create desserts that are both elegant and approachable.

Zippulas, Sardinian-style doughnuts, are a beloved treat during Carnival season, their golden, spiral-shaped forms a symbol of indulgence and celebration. Made from a soft dough of flour, eggs, and yeast, often flavored with orange zest or a touch of anise, zippulas are fried until crisp on the outside and tender on the inside. Once cooked, they are dusted generously with sugar, creating a sweet, crunchy coating that enhances their flavor. These doughnuts are often enjoyed warm, their light, airy texture making them irresistible. The process of making zippulas is often a communal activity, with families and friends gathering to prepare, fry, and eat them together. They embody the spirit of Sardinian festivals, where food becomes a way of bringing people together to share joy and laughter.

Pistiddu, a lesser-known but deeply traditional Sardinian dessert, is a filled pastry that reflects the island's agricultural heritage. The dough, made from semolina and lard, is rolled thin and filled with a mixture of cooked wine must, honey, and spices such as cinnamon or nutmeg. Once filled and sealed, the pastries are baked until golden and often decorated with intricate designs made by pinching or scoring the dough. Pistiddu is especially common in the Barbagia region, where it is prepared for special occasions and religious festivals. The filling, rich and slightly tangy, contrasts beautifully with the crisp, buttery crust, creating a dessert that is as satisfying as it is unique. It is a testament to Sardinia's creativity in using every part of its agricultural resources, turning even the byproducts of winemaking into something extraordinary.

The role of honey in Sardinian desserts cannot be overstated, as it serves as both a sweetener and a flavor enhancer in many traditional recipes. Sardinia's wildflower honey is particularly prized for its complex flavors, which vary depending on the season and the types of flowers in bloom. Strawberry tree honey, or miele di corbezzolo, is a Sardinian specialty with a distinctively bitter-sweet taste that sets it apart from other honeys. This honey is often used in desserts like seadas or drizzled over ricotta cheese for a simple yet exquisite treat. The use of honey in Sardinian sweets is a reflection of the island's reliance on natural, local ingredients and its commitment to preserving traditional flavors.

The art of making Sardinian sweets is often a family affair, with recipes passed down through generations and techniques taught from parent to child. Many Sardinians still prepare these desserts by hand, using methods that have remained unchanged for centuries. This dedication to tradition is evident in the care and precision that go into every step, from selecting the best almonds or honey to shaping each pastry with meticulous attention to detail. Visiting Sardinia and experiencing these desserts firsthand offers a glimpse into the island's culinary soul, where food is not just sustenance but a form of expression and a connection to the past.

Sardinian sweets and pastries are more than just a way to end a meal; they are a celebration of the island's culture, its landscapes, and its people. Each dessert, whether it's a warm, honeyed seadas or a chewy, almond-rich amaretto, carries with it the flavors of Sardinia and the stories of those who created it. To taste these treats is to experience the essence of the island, its ability to find beauty in simplicity, and its unwavering commitment to preserving the traditions that make it unique. Sardinia's sweet offerings are a testament to the power of food to bring people together, to honor the past, and to create moments of joy that linger long after the last bite.

The Best Local Markets and Food Festivals

Sardinia's local markets and food festivals are vibrant, sensory-filled experiences that offer a window into the island's rich culinary traditions, agricultural bounty, and deep-seated sense of community. Across the island, markets bustle with energy, their stalls laden with fresh produce, artisanal goods, and an array of Sardinian delicacies that speak to the heart of its culture. Food festivals, on the other hand, are joyful celebrations of local ingredients and age-old recipes, often tied to religious or seasonal events. Together, these markets and festivals form an essential part of life in Sardinia, where food is not just sustenance but a way of preserving heritage, fostering connections, and celebrating the land's abundance.

The weekly markets in Sardinia are a cornerstone of daily life, where locals gather to shop, socialize, and share stories. Among these, the San Benedetto Market in Cagliari stands out as one of the largest and most renowned. Occupying an expansive two-story building, this market is a feast for the senses, with its lower floor dedicated entirely to seafood. The variety is astonishing—gleaming fish of every size, plump clams and mussels, vivid red prawns, and even the occasional octopus still wriggling in its container. Upstairs, the atmosphere shifts as vendors display an abundance of fruits, vegetables, and regional specialties, from wheels of pecorino cheese to jars of wildflower honey. Visiting San Benedetto is more than a shopping trip; it's an immersion into Sardinia's culinary DNA, where the freshest ingredients form the backbone of the island's cuisine.

In the northern town of Alghero, the Mercato Civico captures the spirit of Sardinia's Catalan-influenced region. This market is smaller but no less vibrant, with a focus on high-quality local produce. Seasonal fruits and vegetables are arranged in colorful displays, while butchers showcase cuts of meat perfect for preparing traditional dishes like porceddu. The fishmongers here are particularly notable, offering fresh catches from the nearby sea, including Alghero's famed lobsters. A stroll through the Mercato Civico provides not just the opportunity to purchase ingredients but the chance to engage with the vendors, who often share cooking tips and stories about their products. It's a reminder that in Sardinia, food is as much about people and relationships as it is about flavor.

Markets in smaller towns, such as the weekly market in Oliena, offer a more intimate experience, where the focus is often on hyper-local goods. Here, you'll find handmade pane carasau, jars of marinated olives, and bottles of wine from nearby vineyards. The atmosphere is relaxed, with a slower pace that allows you to appreciate the craftsmanship behind each product. These smaller markets are also the best places to discover Sardinia's unique herbs and spices, such as myrtle leaves used in the production of the island's famous mirto liqueur. Shopping at a local market like Oliena's feels like stepping into a slice of Sardinian life, where tradition and community take center stage.

While markets offer a glimpse into the everyday culinary world of Sardinia, food festivals take this experience to another level, transforming local ingredients into the stars of grand celebrations. One of the most famous is the Sagra del Redentore in Nuoro, held annually at the end of August. While the festival is primarily religious, honoring the statue of Christ the Redeemer, its accompanying food stalls and communal meals are a highlight. Traditional dishes like culurgiones, handmade pasta stuffed with potatoes and pecorino cheese, are prepared in abundance, alongside roasted meats and local desserts. The festival is a sensory overload of flavors, colors, and sounds, with music and dancing adding to the festive atmosphere. It's a chance not only to taste the best of Sardinian cuisine but to see how deeply food is woven into the island's cultural fabric.

Another unmissable event is the Sagra del Torrone in Tonara, a mountain village famous for its nougat. Held every Easter, this festival celebrates the art of torrone-making, with demonstrations of the process using large copper pots and wooden paddles. The air is thick with the scent of honey and toasted nuts as visitors sample different varieties of torrone, from soft and chewy to richly flavored with almonds or walnuts. The festival also features other local treats, including pistiddu, a filled pastry made with wine must and honey. Attending the Sagra del Torrone is a sweet reminder of Sardinia's ability to create culinary masterpieces from simple, natural ingredients.

In the coastal town of Carloforte, the Girotonno festival pays homage to the island's rich tuna fishing heritage. Held in early summer, this event is a celebration of bluefin tuna, with chefs from around the world competing to create innovative dishes using this prized ingredient. Beyond the culinary competitions, the festival features tastings, cooking demonstrations, and even boat tours to learn about traditional tuna fishing methods. Tuna is prepared in every imaginable way, from raw carpaccio to hearty stews, showcasing its versatility and importance to the Carloforte community. The Girotonno is more than just a food festival; it's a testament to the deep connection between Sardinians and the sea.

The autumn months bring the Cortes Apertas in the Barbagia region, a series of open-house events where villages invite visitors to explore their traditions, crafts, and, of course, cuisine. Each village highlights its specialties, whether it's the hearty zuppa gallurese in Gallura or the smoky flavors of Fiore Sardo cheese in the mountain towns. These events are an opportunity to taste Sardinia's most authentic dishes in their place of origin, often prepared by locals using recipes passed down through generations. The Cortes Apertas are as much about storytelling as they are about food, with each bite offering a deeper understanding of the region's history and way of life.

The role of wine in Sardinian markets and festivals cannot be overlooked, as it is often the perfect complement to the island's cuisine. Many events feature wine tastings, where local producers showcase their Vermentino, Cannonau, and Carignano wines. The Calici di Stelle, held in various locations during the summer, is a particularly magical experience, combining wine tasting with stargazing. Set in vineyards or historic squares, this event pairs Sardinia's finest wines with the beauty of its night skies, creating an atmosphere that is both romantic and celebratory. Markets, too, often have stalls dedicated to local wines, offering visitors the chance to bring home a bottle of Sardinia's terroir.

What makes Sardinia's markets and festivals truly special is the sense of community that permeates every interaction. Vendors greet customers by name, families gather to share meals, and visitors are welcomed as if they were old friends. This warmth and openness create an atmosphere where food becomes more than just a product—it becomes a way of connecting people. Whether you're bargaining for the perfect wedge of pecorino at a market or sharing a plate of fregola con arselle at a festival, the experience is enriched by the relationships you build and the stories you hear.

The importance of seasonality is evident in every market and festival, with offerings that change depending on the time of year. Spring brings artichokes, wild asparagus, and tender lamb, while summer overflows with tomatoes, melons, and fresh seafood. Autumn is the season of chestnuts, wild mushrooms, and robust red wines, while winter highlights citrus fruits, hearty stews, and the sweet richness of seadas. This close connection to the land and its rhythms ensures that Sardinian cuisine remains vibrant and rooted in its natural environment.

For those visiting Sardinia, exploring its markets and food festivals is not just an opportunity to taste its cuisine but a chance to immerse yourself in its culture. These experiences offer a deeper understanding of the island's traditions, its people, and the pride they take in their culinary heritage. From the lively chaos of a bustling market to the joyful celebrations of a festival, Sardinia invites you to savor its flavors, its stories, and its enduring sense of community. It is in these moments, surrounded by the sights, smells, and tastes of the island, that you truly come to understand the soul of Sardinia.

CONCLUSION: YOUR SARDINIAN ADVENTURE AWAITS

Reflecting on Sardinia's Magic

Sardinia is a land that lingers in the soul long after you have left its shores. Its magic is not loud or ostentatious but rather woven into the fabric of its landscapes, its traditions, and the quiet resilience of its people. To reflect on Sardinia is to remember the scent of wild myrtle carried on the wind, the taste of sun-ripened tomatoes bursting with sweetness, and the sound of waves lapping gently against ancient cliffs. It is a place where time seems to stretch and bend, where the past and present coexist in harmony, and where every corner holds a story waiting to be discovered. Sardinia's magic is not something that can be rushed or consumed in haste; it is something you absorb, slowly and deeply, until it becomes a part of you.

The natural beauty of Sardinia is undeniable, and it is often the first thing that captivates those who visit. The island's coastline is a masterpiece of contrasts, with its rugged cliffs plunging into turquoise waters, hidden coves accessible only by boat, and stretches of white sand that feel untouched by time. The beaches of Costa Smeralda, with their crystalline waters and luxury yachts, offer a glimpse of opulence, while the secluded shores of Cala Luna or Cala Goloritzé are havens of tranquility and raw beauty. Inland, Sardinia reveals a different side of itself—a world of rolling hills, ancient oak forests, and sun-drenched plains dotted with wildflowers. The Gennargentu mountains rise dramatically, their peaks often shrouded in mist, creating an otherworldly atmosphere that feels far removed from the modern world. Sardinia's landscapes are not simply beautiful; they are alive, pulsating with the energy of an island that has stood steadfast against the passage of time.

Walking through Sardinia's villages, it becomes clear that the island's magic extends far beyond its physical beauty. Each village has its own character, shaped by its history, its people, and the traditions that have been preserved through the generations. In Barbagia, the heart of Sardinia, the mountain villages are a testament to the island's unyielding spirit. The stone houses of Orgosolo are adorned with murals that tell stories of struggle, resistance, and hope, offering a glimpse into the soul of its inhabitants. In contrast, the coastal town of Bosa, with its pastel-colored houses lining the River Temo, exudes a sense of whimsy and charm. Wandering through the narrow streets, you might encounter an elderly woman weaving baskets from reeds, her hands moving with the practiced ease of someone who has mastered her craft. These villages remind you that Sardinia's magic is not just in its natural splendor but in the lives and traditions of its people.

History is etched into every corner of Sardinia, its ancient roots visible in the countless nuraghi that dot the landscape. These mysterious stone structures, built thousands of years ago, are a testament to the ingenuity and resilience of the Nuragic civilization. Su Nuraxi di Barumini, the most famous of these sites, offers a glimpse into a world that predates written history, its circular towers standing as silent witnesses to the passage of millennia. But it is not just the grand monuments that tell Sardinia's story—sometimes, it is in the smaller, quieter places. The Domus de Janas, or "House of Fairies," are rock-cut tombs that speak to the island's ancient beliefs and rituals, while the Phoenician ruins of Tharros reveal Sardinia's role as a crossroads of civilizations. Sardinia's history is not confined to museums or textbooks; it is alive, woven into the very fabric of the island and its people.

Food and drink are an inseparable part of Sardinia's magic, offering a sensory connection to the island's land and sea. The flavors of Sardinia are bold yet uncomplicated, reflecting the island's agricultural and pastoral heritage. A simple plate of malloreddus, tiny ridged pasta often served with a saffron-infused tomato sauce, speaks volumes about the island's culinary traditions. The cheeses of Sardinia, from the creamy pecorino fresco to the sharp and aged pecorino sardo, are a testament to the skill and dedication of the island's shepherds. And then there is the bread—pane carasau, paper-thin and crisp, or pane frattau, softened with broth and layered with tomato sauce and a poached egg. Each dish tells a story, not just of the ingredients but of the people who have cultivated and prepared them for generations. Sardinia's wines, particularly the robust Cannonau and the crisp Vermentino, are the perfect companions to these meals, their flavors capturing the essence of the island's terroir.

The festivals and celebrations of Sardinia are moments when its magic comes alive in its most vibrant form. Whether it is the haunting chants of the Tenores di Bitti during a religious procession or the joyous chaos of Carnival in Tempio Pausania, these events are a window into the island's soul. The Sagra del Redentore in Nuoro, with its parade of traditional costumes and communal feasts, is not just a celebration but a declaration of Sardinian identity. These festivals are a reminder that Sardinia is a place where tradition is not just remembered but lived, where the past is not a distant memory but a vital part of the present.

At the heart of Sardinia's magic are its people—warm, welcoming, and fiercely proud of their island. There is a sense of authenticity in the way Sardinians approach life, a quiet strength that comes from living in harmony with their land and their history. It is in the shepherd who rises before dawn to tend his flock, the fisherman who knows the rhythms of the sea as if they were an extension of himself, and the artisan who pours their soul into every piece they create. Sardinians are deeply connected to their roots, yet they are also open and generous, eager to share their island's wonders with those who come to visit. In their stories, their songs, and their laughter, you can feel the beating heart of Sardinia.

Reflecting on Sardinia's magic is not just about recalling its landscapes, its food, or its traditions; it is about remembering the way it makes you feel. Sardinia has a way of grounding you, of reminding you of the beauty in simplicity and the strength in resilience. It is a place that invites you to slow down, to savor each moment, and to connect with something deeper than yourself. Sardinia is not a destination to be checked off a list; it is a place to be experienced, to be felt, and to be carried with you long after you leave. Its magic is quiet yet profound, a gentle reminder that some of the most extraordinary things in life are also the simplest. Sardinia stays with you, not as a memory but as a part of who you are, a piece of its magic woven into your own story.

Share Your Experience: Tips for Future Travelers

Traveling to Sardinia is an unforgettable experience, but the island's charm lies in the details, the small moments that can only be fully appreciated when you take the time to prepare and immerse yourself in its culture. Sharing your experience with others who plan to visit can help them uncover even more of what makes Sardinia special. Whether it's advice on navigating its winding roads, cultural customs to keep in mind, or tips for finding the best hidden gems, every detail contributes to making someone else's journey as enriching and magical as possible. Sardinia is not a destination that can be experienced at a glance—it demands exploration, patience, and curiosity. For future travelers, a few practical insights can make all the difference when planning their adventure.

Understanding the seasons is crucial when planning a trip to Sardinia. The island offers a vastly different experience depending on the time of year. Summer, from late June through August, is the peak tourist season, with warm weather, lively beaches, and bustling towns. However, these months also bring crowds and higher prices, particularly in popular areas like Costa Smeralda or Alghero. If your goal is to enjoy Sardinia's pristine beaches, this is the time to visit, but it's essential to book accommodation and transportation well in advance. For those who prefer a quieter experience, the shoulder seasons of May and September are ideal. During these months, the weather remains pleasant, the sea is warm enough for swimming, and the crowds thin out, allowing for a more relaxed pace. Winter, while colder and quieter, offers a unique charm, particularly in the rural areas and mountains, where you can experience Sardinia's festivals, hearty cuisine, and traditional lifestyle without the influx of tourists.

Transportation is another critical consideration. Sardinia is a large island, and its beauty lies in its diversity, from the coastal cliffs to the rolling interior hills. Public transportation, while available, can be limited in terms of routes and schedules, especially in more remote areas. Renting a car is often the best way to explore the island, giving you the freedom to venture off the beaten path and discover places that might otherwise be inaccessible. Driving in Sardinia, however, comes with its own set of challenges. The roads can be narrow, winding, and occasionally steep—particularly in mountainous regions like Barbagia—so patience and caution are necessary. Make sure to familiarize yourself with local traffic rules, and if you're exploring smaller villages, be prepared for cobblestone streets and limited parking. For those who prefer not to drive, organized tours or hiring a local guide can provide an alternative way to experience Sardinia's highlights without the stress of navigating unfamiliar terrain.

Accommodations in Sardinia range from luxurious resorts to charming agriturismi (farm stays), and choosing the right one can significantly enhance your trip. If you're drawn to the glamour and sophistication of Sardinia, the resorts along Costa Smeralda offer world-class amenities, private beaches, and stunning views of the Mediterranean. On the other hand, those seeking a more authentic and immersive experience should consider staying in an agriturismo. These family-run establishments, often located in the countryside, provide cozy lodging and the opportunity to enjoy home-cooked meals made with locally sourced ingredients. Many agriturismi also offer activities like wine tastings, cooking classes, or guided tours of the surrounding area, giving you a deeper connection to the land and its traditions. For budget-conscious travelers, guesthouses, hostels, and small hotels in towns like Cagliari, Oristano, or Nuoro provide comfortable and affordable options.

Food is an integral part of any Sardinian adventure, and knowing where and what to eat can elevate your journey. While restaurants and trattorias are plentiful, some of the most memorable meals can be found in small, family-run establishments or even at local festivals. Sardinia's cuisine is deeply rooted in its agricultural and pastoral heritage, so don't miss the chance to try traditional dishes like porceddu, culurgiones, or fregola con arselle. Fresh seafood is abundant along the coast, with dishes like spaghetti ai ricci di mare (sea urchin pasta) offering a true taste of the Mediterranean. If you're visiting during a festival, the food stalls are a must, serving everything from seadas to roasted chestnuts, depending on the season. Markets, too, are a fantastic place to sample local specialties—don't hesitate to ask vendors for recommendations or tips on how to enjoy their products. And of course, pair your meals with Sardinian wines like Cannonau or Vermentino to complete the experience.

Connecting with locals is perhaps the most rewarding aspect of traveling in Sardinia. The island's residents are known for their warmth and hospitality, and they are often eager to share their stories, traditions, and recommendations. A simple conversation with a shopkeeper, a farmer, or a guide can lead to unexpected discoveries, from hidden beaches to little-known historical sites. While many Sardinians speak Italian, and some speak English, learning a few words or phrases in Sardinian or Italian can go a long way in building rapport and showing respect for the local culture. Don't be afraid to ask questions or show curiosity—most locals are proud of their heritage and happy to share it with visitors who demonstrate genuine interest.

Packing wisely is another key to a successful Sardinian adventure. The island's climate can vary significantly depending on the region and time of year, so it's important to be prepared for both warm days and cooler evenings, especially if you plan to explore the mountains. Comfortable footwear is essential for navigating cobblestone streets, hiking trails, or rocky beaches. If you're visiting in summer, don't forget essentials like sunscreen, a hat, and a reusable water bottle to stay hydrated in the heat. For beachgoers, a lightweight towel, swimwear, and snorkeling gear can enhance your enjoyment of Sardinia's crystalline waters. In the cooler months, layers and a waterproof jacket are advisable, particularly if you're venturing into higher elevations.

Budgeting for Sardinia requires some advance planning, as prices can vary widely depending on the season and location. While the island is often associated with luxury travel, it is entirely possible to experience its beauty and culture on a more modest budget. Shopping at markets, eating at local trattorias, and staying in guesthouses or agriturismi are just a few ways to keep costs down while immersing yourself in Sardinian life. If you plan to visit multiple attractions, consider purchasing a combined ticket or pass, as these often provide discounts for museums, archaeological sites, and guided tours. Additionally, many of Sardinia's most stunning features—its beaches, mountains, and villages—can be enjoyed for free, making it a destination where natural beauty is accessible to all.

Respecting Sardinia's environment and culture is essential for preserving its magic for future travelers. The island's ecosystems, from its marine reserves to its inland forests, are fragile and require care and attention. When visiting beaches, avoid leaving trash behind, and refrain from taking sand, shells, or stones as souvenirs. Stick to marked trails when hiking to protect the flora and fauna, and support sustainable tourism initiatives whenever possible. Cultural respect is equally important—dress modestly when visiting churches or religious sites, and be mindful of local customs and traditions. Sardinia is a place where time-honored ways of life still thrive, and respecting these practices is a way of showing appreciation for the island and its people.

Sharing your experience with other travelers, whether through stories, photos, or recommendations, is a way of keeping Sardinia's magic alive. Every journey is unique, and your insights can inspire others to explore the island in their own way. Whether it's a hidden cove you stumbled upon, a meal that left you speechless, or a conversation that gave you a deeper understanding of Sardinian culture, these moments are worth sharing. They not only help future travelers but also ensure that Sardinia's beauty, traditions, and spirit continue to be celebrated by all who visit. Sardinia is not just a place; it is an experience that grows richer with every story told and every memory cherished.

BONUS 1: ESSENTIAL PHRASES FOR YOUR DAILY TRAVEL NEEDS IN SARDINIA

BONUS 2: PRINTABLE TRAVEL JOURNAL

BONUS 3: 10 TIPS "THAT CAN SAVE THE DAY" ON YOUR TRIP IN SARDINIA

Printed in Great Britain
by Amazon

59635218R00116